ANTONIO BUERO-VALLEJO

In the Burning Darkness

En la ardiente oscuridad

ANTONIO BUERO-VALLEJO

In the Burning Darkness

En la ardiente oscuridad

Translation, Introduction and Notes by

Philip G. Johnston

Antonio Buero-Vallejo (1949).

For Jackie ("Juana"),

with gratitude and love,

por siempre jamás

*Y la luz en las tinieblas resplandece; mas las tinieblas no la
comprendieron.*

"And the light shines in the darkness; but the
darkness did not understand it."

(John 1:5)

*La sombra es el nidal íntimo, incandescente,
la visible ceguera puesta sobre quien ama.
Provoca los abrazos íntima, ciegamente,
y recoge en sus cuevas cuanto la luz derrama.*

"Shadow is the intimate haunt, burning vividly,
the visible blindness placed on whomsoever is in love.
It prompts embraces quietly and blindly,
and gathers in its caves the overflow from light above."

(Miguel Hernández, *The Shadow's Son*)[1]

Aris & Phillips
is an imprint of
Oxbow Books, Oxford, UK

© Text Herederos of Antonio Buero Vallejo, 2000
© Translation, introduction and notes P. G. Johnston, 2010
First printed 2010. Reprinted 2013

ISBN   978-0-85668-843-0

A CIP record for this book is available from the British Library

This book is available direct from

Oxbow Books, Oxford, UK
Phone: 01865-241249; Fax: 01865-794449

and

The David Brown Book Company
PO Box 511, Oakville, CT 06779, USA
Phone: 860-945-9329; Fax: 860-945-9468

or from our website

www.oxbowbooks.com

Cover image: Self portrait of Antonio Buero-Vallejo (circa 1948)

Printed and bound by CPI Group (UK) Ltd, Croydon, CR0 4YY

CONTENTS

TRANSLATOR'S NOTE

At least some part of my belief that this play has a broad, universal appeal stemmed from my – initially purely hypothetical – view that the text would not be really difficult to translate into English and that the translator's intervention, as a cultural mediator, would not be required too often. That view remains largely unchanged after the fact. There are only a few instances where Buero-Vallejo's Spanish is very difficult to render into decent English: one occurs in Act I when Mikey invites the girls to gossip about the boys in their absence and uses an antique reference to a swordsman's sheath (*"tahalí"*) as well as a colloquial Spanish expression *"cortar un traje"* (literally, "to cut a suit"); another, less difficult perhaps, figures further on in the same Act when Jane warns Mikey to be careful about what he says and does, exclaiming proverbially: *"Hay moros en la costa..."* – the translation "walls have ears..." loses out on the historical perspective of centuries of Spanish fear of Moorish (re-)invasion, but does protect the modern reader from the potentially racist overtones of the original phrase in Spanish. Sometimes the subtlety of an expression in the playwright's Spanish has to be sacrificed, as when Mrs P. announces in Act III *"Ignacio se ha matado"*: the English "Iggy's been killed" is largely accurate, but forgoes one tantalising reflexive possibility of the verb *"matarse"*, which is "to kill oneself". Other linguistic challenges are more easily met: the Centre's insistence on the euphemistic *"invidente"* (as opposed to the common *"ciego"*) and *"vidente"* to refer to the blind and the sighted respectively are rendered as "non-seers" (awkward and technical-sounding in perhaps the same way as *"invidente"* is in Spanish) and "seers" (keeping the pun of the original Spanish, meaning someone who can see or has second sight). The perennial difficulty of accounting for the formal – informal (*"Usted"* – *"Tú"* and so on) distinctions in Spanish does not arise here, since, in all instances, the undistinguished "you" in English is perfectly accurate and acceptable – even in, for example, the intensity of the almost Oedipal confrontation between Mrs P. and Charles near the end of Act III, since they never fail to maintain their linguistic formality when speaking to each other.

Because this play is so profoundly metaphorical (not to say, allegorical) in its thrust, and because Buero-Vallejo wrote in that way, at least partly, to avoid the censor's expunging pen, the best approach to translating it surely has to be one that is as faithful and literal as is possible. As noted elsewhere, there is a marked linguistic consistency to aspects of the original Spanish, whether that be in the speech of the defenders of the Centre's régime and in that of its inmates, or in that of its chief detractor, Iggy: so, trite catch-phrases such as *"moral de acero"* or Iggy's cynical insistence on exposing the air of false happiness, *"absurdamente feliz"* and so on, are played with as straight a translator's bat as possible. The author's emphasis on light/darkness and sight/blindness imagery is approached similarly: in, for example, the rendering of the play's title itself, Iggy's reiterative *"¡Quiero ver!"* ("I want to see"), and the Establishment's view of him as a *"contagio"* ("contagion"). Even Buero-Vallejo's foibles – linguistic and otherwise – are consciously preserved and respected in this version: his finicky stage directions, for instance, and his fondness for the inclusion of lengthy adverbs in these. Lastly, in this respect, the very rhetorical nature of some of the speeches is also reproduced as faithfully as possible: Iggy's exchanges with Charles, and even Mrs P.'s final speech, are cases in point.

The aim of this translator is to produce a free-flowing, comprehensible and quite modern-sounding version, in an English which – although almost certainly and inevitably of a Hiberno-bent in some specific instances – cannot generally be said to be overly inclined towards one side of the Atlantic Ocean or the other. The hurried, excited speech of young people, who might be said to be just "hanging out" for swathes of the play, is rendered into English by, *inter alia*, use of abbreviations ("didn't", "wouldn't", "wasn't") and of modern idiom ("blubbering", "big flirt" and so on); sometimes the speech of their elders is slightly slower and certainly more aged: "love birds…cooing…telling off".

Of course no translator is immune to a little cultural mediation on behalf of his putative readers; so although this 50-something translator remembers a *"fumadero"* ("smoking room") in his *alma mater*, the equivalent *locus* in this play has been transmuted into a "common room". This exemplifies a translator's decision that has been shaped by the awareness of what – in this health-conscious age – is now considered unthinkable. It is however still conceivable that young people might smoke; hence the later, untouched references to "cigarettes" and "ashtrays", all of which could amount to a Health and Safety and legal nightmare for potential directors of this play in translation.

The only major translation engineering in this version of Buero-Vallejo's play is in the rendering into English of the cast's names. To translate "Don Pablo" and "Doña Pepita" as "Mr Paul" and "Mrs Fran(ces)" was simply too Dickensian-sounding: so they have been re-named as the more plausible "Mr and Mrs P" (although we know, from Act I, that their forenames are "Paul" and "Fran(ces)"). "Carlos" had to stay as "Charles", because he is a fairly formal (even upper-crust) type; but his girlfriend "Juana" was not seen as a "Joan" (too Maid of Orléans) or a "Joanna" (not enough associations of any kind), but rather as a straight and sound (if not, plain) "Jane". The (anti-) hero "Ignacio" (in spite of his nominal Jesuitical associations) needed a little more "street cred" than "Ignatius" can afford, and finds it with "Iggy" (not "Pop", but nearly). "Elisa", "Andrés", "Pedro", "Lolita" and "Alberto" simply required versions of their names in English with contemporary resonance. "Miguelín" could have been a "Mickey", but, since this rendition of the play into English will hopefully be read and performed beyond the shores of the translator's native island, he is a more international – but still familiar – "Mikey".

One final note: following a practice suggested by the late playwright himself, his double surname, when used in the English-language context of a translation of his work, is hyphenated: Antonio Buero-Vallejo.

Lastly: my thanks to Carlos Buero, Clare Litt, Val Lamb, Tara Evans, Jonathan Thacker and Jackie Johnston for an array of practical help and moral support.

Philip G. Johnston
Dublin 2010

INTRODUCTION

Arguably Spain's leading playwright of the twentieth century, Antonio Buero-Vallejo, who was born in Guadalajara on 29 September 1916 – the son of a military man , Francisco Buero, and of María del Carmen Cruz Vallejo – published thirty original plays. He married the actress Victoria Rodríguez in 1959, and the couple had two sons: Carlos (in 1960) and Enrique (in 1961; RIP). The playwright – often simply referred to as Buero – died on 29 April 2000.

As a young man, Buero-Vallejo studied Art in Madrid's *Escuela de Bellas Artes*. Although *Historia de una escalera* (*Story of a Stairway*) was his first play performed in public (in 1949), *En la ardiente oscuridad* (*In the Burning Darkness*) was, in fact, the first play he wrote – apparently over a few weeks in August 1946. He re-wrote a definitive version of the text in 1950, and it was premiered in the *Teatro María Guerrero* in Madrid on 1 December 1950. The seminal, and lasting, significance of this play was confirmed when an extract from it was read over Buero-Vallejo's grave on the day of his burial in Madrid's *La Paz* cemetery.

Had fate – or the Francoist authorities – decreed differently, Antonio Buero-Vallejo, who was involved on the vanquished Republican side in the Spanish Civil War (1936–39), might never have been heard of in the context of Spanish theatre: for membership of a clandestine cell aiming to reorganise the Spanish Communist Party and to overthrow the Francoist régime he was sentenced to death in January 1940, he then had that judgement commuted to one of thirty years' imprisonment in October of the same year, and served some six years in various prisons before his release in February 1946.

In an interview given in 1973 Buero-Vallejo described *In the Burning Darkness* as a work "*cargada de futuro*" (literally, "loaded with future"), and that observation points the way to why it is being translated now. Although it emerged in 1950 onto a dreary and trivial theatre scene in Francoist Spain, its themes, such as blindness and anxiety of an alienated protagonist, can speak to modern audiences and have a universal, rather that merely parochially Spanish, resonance. It poses a transcendental question about whether or not violence can ever be justified. Its setting

Buero-Vallejo and his wife, the actress Victoria Rodriguez, on their wedding day, 5 March 1959.

in a *"moderno centro de enseñanza"* ("modern teaching centre") could be said to symbolise simply itself, or Spain under Franco (indeed, any country under dictatorship), or the human condition. The play operates on literal, political and philosophical levels. It is an allegory whose significance did not expire with Francisco Franco's death in November 1975, since, for example, many modern workplaces propagate Political Correctness, Team Building, cynical uses of carrot and stick philosophies not dissimilar to those seen in this "centre".

New readers of Buero-Vallejo's work should bear in mind that the playwright wrote this text – as was the case with many of his subsequent plays – against a backcloth of censorship. (The censors, it must be said, were often more interested in detecting offensive blasphemy and sexual innuendo than in uncovering subversive political messages.). With considerable commercial success and thanks to a can-do, *"posibilista"* ("possiblist") approach to dealing with those peering over his shoulder, Buero managed to write his way around the censors to produce plays of social realism with overtones of political allegory. With *In the Burning Darkness* Buero, writing from the standpoint of an ethical Left-winger, describes a teaching centre (for young people who are blind) where a false unity is maintained by a mixture of fear, coercion and diversion (Rome had bread and circuses, Franco's Spain had bullfighting and Real Madrid to divert and entertain the masses), where, when persuasion fails, violence is resorted to, and where "education" is seen to play a part in the régime's ideological structures and to encourage the acceptance of plausible and palatable myths.

The teaching centre's myths are challenged by the play's principal protagonist Iggy who, although blind like his classmates, is immediately seen to be different from the others because he carries a cane. The three-act play's action unfolds over a morning (Act I), an afternoon (Act II) and an evening (Act III) over an indeterminate number of months. Initially his classmates – led by his eventual antagonist Charles – are comforting and sympathetic towards Iggy, and his father is happy to leave his son in such a fine establishment; but as Act I progresses, and Iggy makes a move on Jane, part of the Centre's golden couple with her boyfriend Charles, he begins to challenge and destabilise the values cherished by the Centre. By Act II, Iggy has usurped Charles' position of moral authority over the others and Charles eventually asks him to abandon his rebellious attitudes for the sake of the greater good. Iggy refuses to conform and the Act ends with Iggy stealing Jane's affections and with Charles in a parlous state. In the final Act Charles and Iggy clash verbally, with the latter resisting the former's entreaties to leave for once and for all. As the director of the Centre and his wife (Mr and Mrs P.) express fears about Iggy's influence over his peers, we are given to understand that, off-stage, Charles manages to kill Iggy, but makes it seem like an accident involving the tower of a toboggan run (one of the many "activities" on offer to the students and designed to divert their attention away from their true condition and to foster the illusion or myth of normality). Ironically, at the end of the play, Iggy's influence is as great in death as it was in life: Charles has begun to dress, walk and – crucially – to talk like the man he saw fit to kill.

The most important characters in this archetypically *Bueriano* drama symbolise much more than might first be apparent. Iggy's father, who is sighted and somewhat ingenuous, only wants the best for his blind son and believes that Mr P.'s Centre can provide this. If we read the play as a political allegory, then he is a sort of UN observer invited to visit a country whose dictator has expressly sanitised reality. Mr P., blind himself, and nominally the dictator, is nonetheless naïve in certain ways, and is very much bolstered by his sighted and manipulative wife Mrs P., who really pulls the strings and who knows, because she witnessed the action, that Charles murdered Iggy – which fact she will, of course, repress for the greater good of the Centre. Mikey, the loudest of the cast of other students, is the court jester who, in classic Existentialist mode, is an "inauthentic existent" who jokes his way through everything, thereby averting his gaze from the reality of his situation. Jane, Charles' girlfriend, appears on stage to a fair degree but contributes little. Apparently convinced by Iggy's revisionist ideas, she ultimately loses no time in returning to Charles' side after the demise of his nemesis. Charles himself is the complete establishment figure, a consummate "firm's man" with a conservative dress sense, a nice, safe girlfriend and an apparently unshakable belief in the Centre and in all that it represents. His initial confidence is eroded by Iggy and he debases both himself and the values he espouses by committing the most heinous crime. Iggy, very much the "*homme engagé*", is an agitator and iconoclast; permanently dressed in black, he is the Jesuitical Black Pope (*Ignatius* Loyola) who issues challenges to received thinking. He is cogent and consistent in his deconstruction of the Centre and its false values and in calling a spade a spade: being blind is a dreadful reality, it is not something that can be compensated for by palatable myths.

Displaying a penchant for paradox, inherited perhaps from two of his literary masters, the novelist and philosopher Miguel de Unamuno (1864–1936) and the poet Antonio Machado (1875–1939), Buero-Vallejo once described great theatre as a "*modo de contemplación activa*" ("means of active contemplation") and, indeed, the text of *In the*

Burning Darkness is constructed around a series of conflicting images: light and darkness, sight and blindness, truth and illusion, and, to some extent, peace and war. The first of these binary opposites is embraced in the play's title and glossed in one of its epigraphs, from the New Testament: "And the light shines in the darkness; but the darkness did not understand it." (John 1:5). Conflict arises from misunderstanding or from failure to understand; and so it is that Charles, Mr P. and the Centre they hold dear fail to come to terms with Iggy's burning desire for sight: "*¡Quiero ver!*" ("I want to see!") is his cry. The blindness explored in the play is multi-layered: on a literal level the text speaks of how difficult life as a blind person can be; even though some might say that Buero only uses that physical deprivation as a convenient pretext or means to a very political end. Symbolically, of course, the blindness described does relate to the blindness of post-Civil War Spain, where anti-democratic abuses were overlooked in much the same way as Mr P. will undoubtedly overlook Charles' murderous assault on Iggy. Crucially, however, that blindness is also moral and philosophical; it equates to mankind's unwillingness to confront the reality of our human condition (we prefer to act inauthentically, as do Charles, Mr P., Mikey *et al.*). In Plato's celebrated cave myth, a man who is chained up in a cave with his back to the outside world but escapes, chooses not to return to the cave for fear that his former companions in activity would kill him over their refusal to accept his account of reality in the world beyond the cave. Iggy tries to make his peers confront the truth of being blind, but the purveyors of illusion, who opt to live with or deny the reality of blindness, remove him from the scene. Christ-like in his martyrdom, Iggy tries to bring a war of salvation to the Centre, but the "dogmatic slumber" of a peaceful and unquestioning existence is chosen. Much of the play's dramatic tension and appeal is derived from Buero's exploration of all of these antinomous concepts. When Iggy slyly and subtly moves some items of furniture on an unsuspecting Charles, who subsequently stumbles around, the drama really takes off: philosophically, it is as though the comforting reassurance of the Cartesian "Cogito" has effectively been reversed by a practising Existentialist, who claims that it is only by acknowledging fully the blindness of the human condition, that one can be free and move on.

The play has therefore some of the hallmarks of an Existentialist text, and is comparable, to some extent, to the theatre of Camus and Sartre in France with their emphasis on authenticity, ethical choice and liberty, However, it is also a tragedy – as the term would have been understood by Antonio Buero-Vallejo, who stated in an interview in 1963 that *"la tragedia no es pesimista"* ("tragedy is not pessimistic"). This "optimistic" tragedy involves real flesh and blood characters caught up in believable conflicts (a recipe there for social theatre) and aims to elicit catharsis in its audience, who should be morally refined and improved through dramatic or aesthetic experience.

One of the tools cleverly exploited by the dramatist in this moralistic play is that of language itself. He tellingly mimics the ways in which régimes elaborate their own approved parlance or euphemisms: and so it is that, for example, the normal word in Spanish for "blind", which is *"ciego"*, is replaced by *"invidente"* ("non-seer" or "non-seeing"). The Centre's language has a consistency to it: Mr P. is the master of the trite, clichéd phrase such as *"moral de acero"* ("morale of steel"). Iggy too is given a notable verbal consistency in his attacks on the false happiness about the place, describing Mr P. as *"absurdamente feliz"* ("absurdly happy"), and his peers as *"envenenados de alegría"* ("poisoned with happiness"), full of *"estúpida alegría"* ("stupid happiness") and prone to taking *"duchas de alegría"* (literally, "showers of happiness").

No small measure of the play's dramatic effect or appeal is derived from the author's use of non-linguistic elements. Music, specifically Beethoven's *Moonlight Sonata* (supposedly inspired by a blind boy) and Grieg's *Peer Gynt*, both underscores the emotions involved and, rather more menacingly, because it is broadcast through loudspeakers in the Centre, evokes what might have been played to people in other confined places, such as prison or concentration camps. The dimming of lights for immersion effect on- and off-stage at a key point in Act III has a shock impact on the audience who, momentarily at least, participate physically as well as psychically in the dilemmas confronting the play's characters. The moving of a couple of pieces of furniture by Iggy in Act II devastates the security of Charles' world. On a micro level, the choice of whether or not to wear a tie, or to dress neatly or sloppily, initially symbolises the conflicting attitudes of Charles and Iggy to authority.

In the Burning Darkness has its weaknesses, as well as its strengths, as a piece of theatre. Among the former would be the relatively poorly drawn female characters: Mrs P. may well be a woman of some substance, but the young female students – Jane included – are largely adjuncts to their male peers in whose putatively patriarchal ambit the crucial action unfolds and the key words are spoken. Frankly, at times, the dialogue in the play and some of the values espoused by some of the characters are trivial and almost soap-operaesque. However, Buero-Vallejo might have argued, the minutiae of boyfriends/girlfriends, who's married to whom and so on, are the stuff of young lives and part of the "Intrahistoria" ("Intrahistory") – to use a phrase from Unamuno of which Buero would have approved – of the broader human story and perhaps reflect, rather cleverly, a sort of "dumbing-down" cultivated by the régime on occasions. It has been argued that the play suffers because its main event – Charles's murder of Iggy – happens off-stage; but, it might be countered, that is how oppressive régimes often remove their most implacable enemies: almost imperceptible, subterfugal "dirty tricks" are a characteristic of state violence against individuals. Occasionally the charge of writing *littérature à thèse* has been laid at Buero-Vallejo's door. Perhaps, indeed, there is something didactic (in a socio-political context) about certain passages in this play; but Buero-Vallejo himself disliked the label "teatro de ideas" ("theatre of ideas") and therefore would not have sought to write exclusively in that mode; some of the younger, more frivolous dialogue might in fact be said to be a deliberate antidote to didactic writing.

One of the facets of the play which could be said to mean that Buero escapes the above charge, and which furthermore may be viewed as one of the dramatic strengths of the text, is the subtle and nuanced drawing of the two principal protagonists, Iggy and Charles. Their characterisation is full of grey areas: Iggy may well be the Existentialist (anti-)hero, but perhaps it could be argued that his general attitude is pessimistic and full of self-pity, that his notion of blindness is archaic, and that the greater good in the Centre would be better served by his leaving altogether or, at least, by his compromising on his principles; Charles, although he is open to criticism for allowing himself to be the unquestioning and sycophantic favourite son of the Centre, might be said to epitomise strength, security and steadfastness and ultimately proves to be magnanimous through embracing Iggy's "vision" of things in the end. Another of the play's strengths surely lies in the wonderfully acrid and dramatic verbal exchanges between those two principal men – exchanges worthy of the most vivid

Buero-Vallejo at home in 1987.

domestic, parliamentary or philosophical debate. The play's effectiveness is also enhanced by those already mentioned plays with light and darkness on stage and in the auditorium, orchestrated by Buero and exemplifying his characteristic mastery of stagecraft. Effective too is the sheer, literal impact of blindness: a stageful of actors, most of whom presumably pretend to be blind, would surely challenge any audience in any era.

Challenging audiences and seeking hopefully to change mind-sets was the stock in trade of Antonio Buero-Vallejo as a dramatist. As he once stated himself: "*Se escribe porque se espera*" ("One writes because one hopes").

SELECT BIBLIOGRAPHY

Principal edition of Antonio Buero-Vallejo's complete works

Buero-Vallejo, Antonio, *Obra Completa*, eds L. Iglesias Feijoo and M. de Paco, Clásicos Castellanos Nueva Serie, 2 vols (Madrid: Espasa-Calpe, 1994).

Edition of play on which this translation is based

Buero-Vallejo, Antonio, *En la ardiente oscuridad*, ed. M. de Paco, Austral Teatro 124, 30th ed. (Madrid: Espasa-Calpe, 2006).

Books and articles (in English)

Anderson, R., "Tragic Conflict and Progressive Synthesis in Buero-Vallejo's *En la ardiente oscuridad*", *Symposium* 29 (nos. 1–2, 1975), 1–12.

Brown, G. G., *A Literary History of Spain: The Twentieth Century*, 2nd ed. (London: Ernest Benn, 1974).

Dixon, V., "The 'immersion-effect' in the Plays of Antonio Buero-Vallejo" in ed. M. de Paco *Estudios sobre Antonio Buero-Vallejo* (Murcia: Murcia University Press, 1984), 159–83.

Edwards, G., *Dramatists in Perspective: Spanish Theatre in the Twentieth Century* (Cardiff: University of Wales Press, 1985).

Gabriele, J. P., "Death and Dying in *En la ardiente oscuridad*", *The USF Language Quarterly*, 26 (nos. 1–2, 1987), 13–16, 19.

Jordan, B., "Blindness and Insight: A Re-reading of Buero-Vallejo's *En la ardiente oscuridad*", *Modern Languages*, 64 (no. 3, 1983), 185–92.

Nicholas, R. L., *The Tragic Stages of Antonio Buero-Vallejo*, Estudios de Hispanófila, Dept of Romance Languages, University of North Carolina (Madrid: Castalia, 1972).

Ruple, J., *Antonio Buero-Vallejo: The First Fifteen Years* (New York: Elises Torres, 1971).

CAST

(in order of speaking)

Lisa	Elisa
Andy	Andrés
Pete	Pedro
Linda	Lolita
Al	Alberto
Charles	Carlos
Jane	Juana
Mikey	Miguel
Hope	Esperanza
Iggy	Ignacio
Mr P.	Don Pablo
Iggy's father	El Padre
Mrs P.	Doña Pepita

A still from the Norwegian production of the play, premiered in Oslo, 12 May 1962. A young Liv Ullman plays Juana.

EN LA ARDIENTE OSCURIDAD

IN THE BURNING DARKNESS

ACTO PRIMERO

Fumadero en un moderno centro de enseñanza: lugar semiabierto de tertulia para el buen tiempo. A la izquierda del foro, portalada que da a la terraza. Al fondo se divisa la barandilla de ésta, bajo la cual se supone el campo de deportes. Las ramas de los copudos árboles que en él hay se abren tras la barandilla, cuajadas de frondoso follaje, que da al ambiente una gozosa claridad submarina. Sobre una liviana construcción de cemento, enormes cristaleras, tras las que se divisa la terraza, separan a ésta de la escena, dejando el hueco de la portalada. En el primer término izquierdo hay un veladorcito y varios sillones y sillas. En el centro, cerca del foro, un sofá y dos sillones alrededor de otro veladorcito. Junto al lateral derecho, otro velador aislado como un sillón. Ceniceros en los tres veladores. Las cristaleras doblan y continúan fuera de escena, a la mitad del lateral izquierdo, formando la entrada de una galería. En el lateral derecho, una puerta.

(*Cómoda y plácidamente sentados, fumando algunos de ellos, vemos allí a ocho jóvenes estudiantes pulcramente vestidos. No obstante su aire risueño y atento, hay algo en su aspecto que nos extraña, y una observación más detenida nos permite comprender que todos son ciegos. Algunos llevan gafas negras, para velar, sin duda, un espectáculo demasiado desagradable a los demás; o, tal vez, por simple coquetería. Son ciegos jóvenes y felices, al parecer; tan seguros de sí mismos que, cuando se levantan, caminan con facilidad y se localizan admirablemente, apenas sin vacilaciones o tanteos. La ilusión de normalidad es, con frecuencia, completa, y el espectador acabaría por olvidar la desgracia física que los aqueja si no fuese por un detalle irreductible que a veces se la hace recordar: estas gentes nunca se enfrentan con la cara de su interlocutor.*
CARLOS y JUANA *ocupan los sillones de la izquierda. Él es un muchacho fuerte y sanguíneo, de agradable y enérgica expresión. Atildado indumento en color claro, cuello duro. Ella es linda y dulce.* ELISA *ocupa el sillón de la derecha. Es una muchacha de físico vulgar y de espíritu abierto, simple y claro. En el sofá están los estudiantes* ANDRÉS, PEDRO y ALBERTO, *y en los sillones contiguos, las estudiantes* LOLITA y ESPERANZA.)

ACT I

A students' common room in a modern teaching centre: a meeting place that can be opened to the outdoors in fine weather. Up-stage Right is a door which opens onto a terrace, whose railings can be seen and under those is the supposed location of the sports field. The branches of its bushy trees are behind the railings, and are full of ample foliage, giving the setting a pleasant, subaqueous clarity. On a light cement framework there are large French windows through which the terrace can be seen and which separate it from the stage, except at the doorway. Down-stage Right there is a small occasional table and some chairs and armchairs. Up Centre are a sofa and two armchairs placed around another small table. At the Left wing of the stage is another, single small table with an armchair. All three tables have ashtrays. The French windows form an angle, continuing off-stage, at the halfway point on the Right wing, creating the entrance to a passage. On the Left wing of the stage there is a door.

(*We see eight neatly-dressed young students sitting comfortably and calmly, some of them smoking. In spite of their cheerful, alert manner, there is something about them which perplexes us, and a closer inspection tells us that they are all blind. Some wear dark glasses, doubtless to conceal a sight that is too unpleasant for others, or perhaps, for sheer effect. These young blind people are seemingly happy, and are so sure of themselves that, when they get up, they walk around easily and find their way wonderfully well, almost without hesitation or fumbling. The illusion of normality is often complete and the spectator would ultimately forget the physical misfortune afflicting them, were it not for one ineluctable detail which at times brings it to mind: these people never look at the face of the person to whom they are talking.*
    CHARLES *and* JANE *are sitting in the armchairs to the Right. He is a strong, fresh-faced boy with a pleasant, energetic look about him. He is immaculately dressed in bright colours, and wears a shirt and tie. She is pretty and sweet.* LISA *sits in the armchair to the Left. She is a plain-looking girl with an open, simple and straightforward nature. On the sofa sit the students* ANDY, PETE *and* AL, *and on the nearby armchairs are* LINDA *and* HOPE.)[2]

ELISA	(*Impaciente.*) ¿Qué hora es, muchachos? (*Casi todos ríen, expansivos, como si hubiesen estado esperando la pregunta.*) No sé por qué os reís. ¿Es que no se puede preguntar la hora? (*Las risas arrecian.*) Está bien. Me callo.
ANDRÉS	Hace un rato que dieron las diez y media.
PEDRO	Y la apertura del curso es a las once.
ELISA	Yo os preguntaba si habían dado ya los tres cuartos.
LOLITA	Hace un rato que nos lo has preguntado por tercera vez.
ELISA	(*Furiosa.*) Pero ¿han dado o no?
ALBERTO	(*Humorístico.*) ¡Ah! No sabemos...
ELISA	¡Sois odiosos!
CARLOS	(*Con ironía.*) Ya está bien. No os metáis con ella. Pobrecilla.
ELISA	¡Yo no soy pobrecilla!
JUANA	(*Dulce.*) Todavía no dieron los tres cuartos, Elisa.

(MIGUELÍN, *un estudiante jovencito y vivaz, que lleva gafas oscuras, porque sabe por experiencia que su vivacidad es penosa cuando las personas que ven la contrastan con sus ojos muertos, aparece por la portalada.*)

ANDRÉS	Tranquilízate. Ya sabes que Miguelín llega siempre a todo con los minutos contados.
ELISA	¿Y quién pregunta por Miguelín?
MIGUEL	(*Cómicamente compungido.*) Si nadie pregunta por Miguelín, lloraré.
ELISA	(*Levantándose de golpe.*) ¡Miguelín!

(*Corre a echarse en sus brazos, mientras los demás acogen al recién llegado con cariñosos saludos. Todos, menos* CARLOS *y* JUANA, *se levantan y se acercan para estrechar su mano.*)

ANDRÉS	¡Caramba, Miguelín!
PEDRO	¡Ya era hora!
LOLITA	¡La tenías en un puño!
ESPERANZA	¿Qué tal te ha ido?
ALBERTO	¿Cómo estás?

(*Sin soltar a* ELISA, MIGUELÍN *avanza decidido hacia el sofá.*)

LISA	(*Impatiently.*) What time is it, guys? (*They almost all laugh, exaggeratedly, as though they had been expecting the question.*) I don't know why you're laughing. Can I not even ask the time? (*The laughter increases.*) Fine. I'll be quiet.
ANDY	Just a short while ago it struck half ten.
PETE	And the opening assembly is at eleven.
LISA	I was asking if it had already struck a quarter to.
LINDA	It was just a moment ago that you asked for the third time.
LISA	(*Angrily.*) But, is that the time, or not?
AL	(*In a humorous tone.*) Ah, we don't know…
LISA	You're hateful, the lot of you!
CHARLES	(*Sarcastically.*) That's enough, don't pick on her. Poor thing!
LISA	I'm not a poor thing!
JANE	(*Sweetly.*) It hasn't struck a quarter to yet, Lisa.

(MIKEY *appears at the doorway; he is a lively young student who wears dark glasses because he knows from experience that his liveliness is hard to take for sighted people when they contrast it with his dead eyes.*)

ANDY	Relax. You know that Mikey always turns up at everything just in the nick of time.
LISA	And who's talking about Mikey?
MIKEY	(*Humorously aggrieved.*) If nobody is talking about Mikey, I'll start crying.
LISA	(*Jumping up.*) Mikey!

(*She hurries to throw herself into his arms, while the others greet the recent arrival warmly. Everyone, except* CHARLES *and* JANE, *gets up and goes over to shake his hand.*)[3]

ANDY	Hey, Mikey!
PETE	It's about time!
LINDA	You had her in a state!
HOPE	How did things go?
AL	How are you? (*Without letting go of* LISA, MIKEY *moves decisively towards the sofa.*)

CARLOS   ¿Ya no te acuerdas de los amigos?

MIGUEL   ¡Carlos! (*Se acerca a darle la mano.*) Y Juana al lado, seguro.

JUANA   Lo has acertado.

(*Le da la mano.*)

MIGUEL   (*Volviendo a coger a* ELISA.) ¡Uf! Creí que no llegaba a la apertura. Lo he pasado formidable, chicos; formidable. (*Se sienta en el sofá con* ELISA *a su lado.* ANDRÉS *se sienta con ellos. Los demás se sientan también.*) ¡Pero tenía unas ganas de estar con vosotros! Es mucha calle la calle, amigos. Aquí se respira. En cuanto he llegado, ¡zas!, el bastón al conserje. «¿Llego tarde?». «Aún faltan veinte minutos». «Bien». Saludos aquí y allá... «¡Miguelín!». «Ya está aquí Miguelín». Y es que soy muy importante, no cabe duda.

(*Risas generales.*)

ELISA   (*Convencida de ello.*) ¡Presumido!

MIGUEL   Silencio. Se prohíbe interrumpir. Continúo. «Miguelín, ¿adonde vas?» «Miguelín, en la terraza está Elisa...»

ELISA   (*Avergonzada, le propina un pellizco.*) ¡Idiota!

MIGUEL   (*Gritando.*) ¡Ay!... (*Risas.*) Continúo. «¿Que a dónde voy? Con mi peña y a nuestro rincón». Y aquí me tenéis. (*Suspira.*) Bueno, ¿qué hacemos que no nos vamos al paraninfo?

(*Intenta levantarse.*)

LOLITA   No empieces tú ahora. Sobra tiempo.

ANDRÉS   (*Reteniéndole.*) Cuenta, cuéntanos de tus vacaciones.

ESPERANZA   (*Batiendo palmas.*) Sí, sí. Cuenta.

ELISA   (*Muy amoscada, batiendo palmas también.*) Sí, sí. Cuéntaselo a la niña.

ESPERANZA   (*Desconcertada.*) ¿Eso qué quiere decir?

ELISA   (*Seca.*) Nada. Que también yo sé batir palmas.

(*Los estudiantes ríen.*)

CHARLES	Have you forgotten your friends already?
MIKEY	Charles! (*He moves to shake his hand.*) With Jane in tow, no doubt.
JANE	Got it in one! (*She extends her hand to him.*)
MIKEY	(*Taking hold of* LISA *again.*) Phew! I thought I wasn't going to make the opening assembly. I've had a great time, guys, a great time. (*He sits on the sofa with* LISA *by his side.* ANDY *sits down with them. The others also sit down.*) But I really wanted to be with you people! It's all go out there. Here you get a breather. As soon as I arrived, wham, gave my stick to the caretaker. 'Am I late?' 'Twenty minutes to go.' 'Great.' Salutations here, there and everywhere... 'Mikey!', 'Mikey's here!' There's no doubt about it, I'm very important. (*General laughter.*)[4]
LISA	(*With conviction.*) Big head!
MIKEY	Quiet. No interruptions. As I was saying... 'Mikey, where are you going?' 'Mikey, Lisa's out on the terrace...'
LISA	(*Embarrassed, pinches him.*) You fool!
MIKEY	(*Crying out.*) Ouch!... (*Laughter.*) As I was saying... 'You want to know where I'm going? To meet my gang and then head to our hang-out.' And here I am. (*He sighs.*) Well then, how come we're not going to the main hall? (*He goes to get up.*)
LINDA	Don't you start now. There's plenty of time.
ANDY	(*Holding him back.*) Tell all, tell us about your holidays.
HOPE	(*Clapping her hands.*) Ooh yes, tell us.
LISA	(*Very cross, clapping as well.*) Ooh yes. Tell the little girl.
HOPE	(*Taken aback.*) What do you mean by that?
LISA	(*Drily.*) Nothing. *I* can clap hands too. (*The students laugh.*)

ESPERANZA   (*Molesta.*) ¡Bah!
MIGUEL   Modérate, Elisa. Los señores quieren que les cuente de
             mis vacaciones. Pues atended.

(*Los chicos se arrellanan, complacidos y dispuestos a oír algo divertido.*
MIGUELÍN *empieza a reírse con zumba.*)

PEDRO   ¡Empieza de una vez!
MIGUEL   Atended. (*Riendo.*) Un día cojo mi bastón para salir a la
             calle, y... (*Se interrumpe. Con tono de sorpresa.*) ¿No
             oís algo?
ANDRÉS   ¡Sigue y no bromees!
MIGUEL   ¡Si no bromeo! Os digo que oigo algo raro. Oigo un
             bastón...
LOLITA   (*Riendo.*) El tuyo, que lo tienes en los oídos todavía.
ELISA   Continúa, tonto...
ALBERTO   No bromea, no. Se oye un bastón.
JUANA   También yo lo oigo.

(*Todos atienden. Pausa. Por la derecha, tanteando el suelo con su bastón
y con una expresión de vago susto, aparece* IGNACIO. *Es un muchacho
delgaducho, serio y reconcentrado, con cierto desaliño en su persona:
el cuello de la camisa desabrochado, la corbata floja, el cabello peinado
con ligereza. Viste de negro, intemporalmente, durante toda la obra.
Avanza unos pasos, indeciso, y se detiene.*)

LOLITA   ¡Qué raro!

(IGNACIO *se estremece y retrocede un paso.*)

MIGUEL   ¿Quién eres?

(*Temeroso,* IGNACIO *se vuelve para salir por donde entró. Después
cambia de idea y sigue hacia la izquierda, rápido.*)

ANDRÉS   ¿No contestas?

(IGNACIO *tropieza con el sillón de* JUANA. *Tiende el brazo y ella toma su
mano.*)

MIGUEL   (*Levantándose.*) ¡Espera, hombre! No te marches.

(*Se acerca a palparle, mientras* JUANA *dice, inquieta:*)

HOPE	(*Annoyed.*) Bah!
MIKEY	Take it easy, Lisa. The ladies and gentlemen want me to tell them about my holidays. So, listen, everybody. (*The boys settle down, happy and ready to hear something amusing.* MIKEY *begins to chuckle.*)
PETE	For God's sake, get on with it!
MIKEY	Pay attention, everyone. (*Laughing.*) One day I grab my stick to hit the street and… (*He stops short, in a surprised tone.*) Don't you hear something?
ANDY	Carry on and stop messing!
MIKEY	I'm not messing. I'm telling you, I hear something strange. I hear a stick tapping…
LINDA	(*Laughing.*) It's your own, you've still got the sound ringing in your ears.
LISA	Go on, you fool…
AL	No, he's not joking. You *can* hear a stick.
JANE	I can hear it too. (*They all perk up. A pause. To the Left, tapping the ground with his cane and wearing a vaguely shocked expression, appears* IGGY. *He is a skinny, serious, intense boy with a certain slovenliness about him: his shirt collar is undone, his tie is loose, his hair is barely combed. Throughout the play he is always dressed in black, whatever the season. He takes a few hesitant steps forward and stops.*)[5]
LINDA	How strange! (IGGY *flinches and steps back.*)
MIKEY	Who are you? (*In fear,* IGGY *turns to leave through where he entered. Then he changes his mind and crosses Right quickly.*)
ANDY	Are you not answering? (IGGY *bumps into* JANE*'s armchair. He stretches out his arm and she takes his hand.*)
MIKEY	(*Getting up.*) Hold on a minute, mate. Don't go away. (*He approaches to touch him, while* JANE *says in worried tones:*)

JUANA   Me ha cogido la mano.... No le conozco.

(IGNACIO *la suelta, y* MIGUELÍN *lo sujeta por un brazo.*)

MIGUEL   Ni yo.

(ANDRÉS *se levanta y se acerca también para cogerle por el otro brazo.*)

IGNACIO   (*Con temor.*) Dejadme.
ANDRÉS   ¿Qué buscas aquí?
IGNACIO   Nada. Dejadme. Yo... soy un pobre ciego.
LOLITA   (*Riendo.*) Te ha salido un competidor, Miguelín.
ESPERANZA.   ¿Un competidor? ¡Un maestro!
ALBERTO   Debe de ser algún gracioso del primer curso.
MIGUEL   Dejádmelo a mí. ¿Qué has dicho que eres?
IGNACIO   (*Asustado.*) Un... ciego.
MIGUEL   ¡Oh, pobrecito, pobrecito! ¿Quiere que le pase a la otra
               acera? (*Los demás se desternillan.*) ¡Largo, idiota! Vete
               a reír de los de tu curso.
ANDRÉS   Realmente, la broma es de muy mal gusto. Anda,
               márchate.

(*Lo empujan.* IGNACIO *retrocede hacia el proscenio.*)

IGNACIO   (*Violento, quizá al borde del llanto.*) ¡Os digo que soy
               ciego!
MIGUEL   ¡Qué bien te has aprendido la palabrita! ¡Largo!

(*Avanzan hacia él, amenazadores.* ALBERTO *se levanta también.*)

IGNACIO   Pero ¿es que no lo veis?
MIGUEL   ¿Cómo?

(JUANA *y* CARLOS, *que comentaban en voz baja el incidente, intervienen.*)

CARLOS   Creo que estamos cometiendo un error muy grande,
               amigos. Él dice la verdad. Sentaos otra vez.
MIGUEL   ¡Atiza!
CARLOS   (*Acercándose con* JUANA *a* IGNACIO.) Nosotros también
               somos... ciegos, como tú dices.
IGNACIO   ¿Vosotros?
JUANA   Todos lo somos. ¿Es que no sabes dónde estás?

JANE	He's taken my hand... I don't know him. (IGGY *lets go of her, and* MIKEY *grabs his arm.*)[6]
MIKEY	Me neither. (ANDY *gets up and comes over to take him by the other arm.*)
IGGY	(*Afraid.*) Let me go.
ANDY	What are you doing here?
IGGY	Nothing. Let me go. I'm just a poor blind guy.[7]
LINDA	(*Laughing.*) You've got competition, Mikey.
HOPE	Competition? This guy's a real artist!
AL	It must be some funny guy from First Year.
MIKEY	Leave him to me! What did you say you were?
IGGY	(*Startled.*) A... blind guy!
MIKEY	Ah, poor chap, poor chap! Would you like me to help you over to the other side of the road? (*The others crack up laughing.*) Go away, you fool! Go and laugh at people in your own year.
ANDY	Seriously, that's joke's in very bad taste. Go on, clear off. (*They push him.* IGGY *goes back towards the proscenium.*)
IGGY	(*Vehemently, perhaps on the verge of tears.*) I'm telling you, I'm blind!
MIKEY	You've learned that little word well! Clear off! (*They move menacingly towards him.* AL *also gets up.*)
IGGY	But, can you not see that I'm blind?
MIKEY	What? (JANE *and* CHARLES, *who were commenting on the incident in hushed tones, intervene.*)
CHARLES	I think we're making a very big mistake here, friends. He's telling the truth. Sit down again.
MIKEY	Oops!
CHARLES	(*Moving with* JANE *towards* IGGY.) We too are... blind, as you say.[8]
IGGY	You?
JANE	We're all blind. Don't you know where you are?

(ELISA *toma del brazo a* MIGUELÍN, *que está desconcertado. Los estudiantes murmuran entre sí.* ANDRÉS *y* PEDRO *vuelven a sentarse. Todos atienden.*)

IGNACIO	Sí lo sé. Pero no puedo creer que seáis... como yo.
CARLOS	(*Sonriente.*) ¿Por qué?
IGNACIO	Andáis con seguridad. Y me habláis... como si me estuvieseis viendo.
CARLOS	No tardarás tú también en hacerlo. Acabas de venir, ¿verdad?
IGNACIO	Sí.
CARLOS	¿Solo?
IGNACIO	No. Mi padre está en el despacho, con el director.
JUANA	¿Y te han dejado fuera?
IGNACIO	El director dijo que saliera sin miedo. Mi padre no quería, pero don Pablo dijo que saliese y que anduviese por el edificio. Dijo que era lo mejor.
CARLOS	(*Protector.*) Y es lo mejor. No tengas miedo.
IGNACIO	(*Con orgullo.*) No lo tengo.
CARLOS	Lo de aquí ha sido un incidente sin importancia. Es que Miguelín es demasiado alocado.
MIGUEL	Dispensa, chico. Todo fue por causa de don Pablo.
ALBERTO	(*Riendo.*) La pedagogía.
MIGUEL	Eso. Te ha aplicado la pedagogía desde el primer minuto. Ya tendrás más encuentros con esa señora. No te preocupes.

(*Se vuelve con* ELISA, *y ambos se sientan en los dos sillones de la izquierda. Se ponen a charlar, muy amartelados.*)

CARLOS	Por esta vez es bastante. Si quieres te volveremos al despacho.
IGNACIO	Gracias. Sé ir yo solo. Adiós.

(*Da unos pasos hacia el foro.*)

CARLOS	(*Calmoso.*) No, no sabes... Por ahí se va a la salida. (*Le coge afectuosamente del brazo y le hace volver hacia la derecha. Pasivo y con la cabeza baja,* IGNACIO *se deja conducir.*) Espérame aquí, Juana. Vuelvo en seguida.
JUANA	Sí.

(LISA *takes the disconcerted* MIKEY *by the arm. The students mutter among themselves.* ANDY *and* PETE *sit down again. They all listen.*)

IGGY	Yes, I know. But I can't believe that you're... like me.
CHARLES	(*Smiling.*) Why not?
IGGY	You walk about confidently. And you talk to me... as if you were seeing me.
CHARLES	You too will soon be doing those things. You've just arrived, haven't you?
IGGY	Yes.
CHARLES	Alone?
IGGY	No, my father's in the office, with the director.
JANE	And they left you outside?
IGGY	The director said that I could go out, no problem. My father didn't want me to, but Mr P. told me to go out and walk around the building. He said it was the best thing.
CHARLES	(*Reassuringly.*) And so it is. Don't be afraid.
IGGY	(*Proudly.*) I'm not.
CHARLES	What happened just now was unimportant. Mikey's too impetuous.
MIKEY	Sorry, mate. It was all because of Mr P.
AL	(*Laughing.*) First lesson in pedagogy!
MIKEY	That's it. From the minute you're here he's applying pedagogical theory.[9] It won't be the last time either. Don't worry. (*He turns with* LISA, *and they sit down on the two armchairs on the Right. They start chatting and canoodling.*)
CHARLES	That's enough for now. If you want, we'll bring you back to the office.
IGGY	No thanks. I can get there by myself. Bye. (*He takes a few steps Up-stage.*)
CHARLES	(*Calmly.*) No, you don't know how... The exit's over this way. (*He takes him gently by the arm and turns him round to the Left. Passively, and with his head bowed,* IGGY *lets himself be led.*) Wait here for me, Jane. I'll be back in a tick.[10]
JANE	Fine.

(*Por la derecha aparecen* EL PADRE DE IGNACIO *y* DON PABLO, *director del centro.* EL PADRE *entra con ansiosa rapidez, buscando a su hijo. Es un hombre agotado y prematuramente envejecido, que viste con mezquina corrección de empleado. Sonriente y tranquilo, le sigue* DON PABLO, *señor de unos cincuenta años, con las sienes grises, en quien la edad no ha borrado un vago aire de infantil lozanía. Su vestido es serio y elegante. Usa gafas oscuras.*)

EL PADRE   Aquí está Ignacio.

DON PABLO   Ya le dije que lo encontraríamos. (*Risueño.*) Y en buena compañía, creo. Buenos días, muchachos. (*A su voz, todos los estudiantes se levantan.*)

ESTUDIANTES Buenos días, don Pablo.

(EL PADRE *se acerca a su hijo y le coge, entre tímido y paternal, por el brazo.* IGNACIO *no se mueve, como si el contacto le disgustase.*)

CARLOS   Ya hemos hecho conocimiento con Ignacio.

JUANA   Carlos se lo llevaba ahora a ustedes.

DON PABLO   (*Al* PADRE.) Como ve, no le ha pasado nada. El chico ha encontrado en seguida amigos. Y de los buenos: Carlos, que es uno de nuestros mejores alumnos, y Juana.

EL PADRE   (*Corto.*) Encantado.

JUANA   El gusto es nuestro.

DON PABLO   Su hijo se encontrará bien entre nosotros, puede estar seguro. Aquí encontrará alegría, buenos compañeros, juegos...

EL PADRE   Sí, desde luego. Pero los juegos... ¡Los juegos que he visto son maravillosos, no hay duda! Nunca pude suponer que los ciegos pudiesen jugar al balón. ¡Y menos, deslizarse por un tobogán tan alto! (*Tímido.*) ¿Cree usted que mi Ignacio podrá hacer esas cosas sin peligro?.

DON PABLO   Ignacio hará eso y mucho más. No lo dude.

EL PADRE   ¿No se caerá?

DON PABLO   ¿Acaso se caen los otros?

EL PADRE   Es que parece imposible que puedan jugar así, sin que haya que lamentar...

DON PABLO   Ninguna desgracia; no, señor. Esas y otras distracciones llevan ya mucho tiempo entre nosotros.

(*To the Left appear* IGGY's *father and* MR P., *the Centre's director. Quickly and anxiously, the father enters looking for his son. He is a tired, prematurely aged man, dressed with the paltry correctness of a clerk. He is followed by a smiling, calm* MR P., *a man of around fifty, with grey temples, in whom age has not erased a slight air of childish freshness. He is dressed in a sober and elegant manner. He wears dark glasses.*)

THE FATHER	Iggy's here.
MR P.	I told you we'd find him. (*Cheerfully.*) And in good company, I believe. 'Morning, everyone. (*On hearing his voice, all the students stand up.*)
STUDENTS	Good morning, Mr P. (*The father goes over to his son and takes him by the arm in a manner somewhere between timid and paternal.* IGGY *does not move, as though this contact bothers him.*)
CHARLES	We've already got to know Iggy.
JANE	Charles was just bringing him round to you.
MR P.	(*To the father.*) As you can see, no harm's come to him. The boy has made friends straight away. And good ones, at that. Charles, who's one of our best students, and Jane.
THE FATHER	(*Awkwardly.*) Pleased to meet you.
JANE	The pleasure's ours.
MR P.	Your son will be fine with us, you can be sure. Here he'll find happiness, good companions, activities…
THE FATHER	Yes, of course. Now the activities… the activities that I've seen are marvellous, no doubt. I would never have imagined that blind people could play ball, never mind tobogganing down that slide from such a height. (*Timidly.*) Do you think that my Iggy will be able to do those things without endangering himself?[11]
MR P.	Iggy will do that and much more. Don't doubt it.
THE FATHER	Won't he fall?
MR P.	Do you think the others fall?
THE FATHER	It seems impossible that they can play like that, without there being…
MR P.	Any mishaps. There are none, Sir. These and other activities have been part of our set-up for a long time.

EL PADRE	Pero todos estos chicos, ¡pobrecillos!, son ciegos. ¡No ven nada!
DON PABLO	En cambio, oyen y se orientan mejor que usted. (*Los estudiantes asienten con rumores.*) Por otra parte... (*Irónico.*), no crea que es muy adecuado calificarlos de pobrecillos. ¿No le parece, Andrés?
ANDRÉS	Usted lo ha dicho.
DON PABLO	¿Y ustedes, Pedro, Alberto?
PEDRO	Desde luego, no. No somos pobrecillos.
ALBERTO	Todo, menos eso.
LOLITA	Si usted nos permite, don Pablo...
DON PABLO	Sí, diga.
LOLITA	(*Entre risas.*) Nada. Que Esperanza y yo pensamos lo mismo.
EL PADRE	Perdonen.
DON PABLO	Perdónenos a nosotros por lo que parece una censura y no es más que una explicación. Los ciegos o, simplemente, los invidentes, como nosotros decimos, podemos llegar donde llegue cualquiera. Ocupamos empleos, puestos importantes en el periodismo y en la literatura, cátedras... Somos fuertes, saludables, sociables... Poseemos una moral de acero. Por lo demás, no son éstas conversaciones a las que ellos estén acostumbrados. (*A los demás.*) Creo que los más listos de ustedes podrían ir ya tomando sitio en el paraninfo. Falta poco para las once. (*Risueño.*) Es un aviso leal.
ANDRÉS	Gracias, don Pablo. Vámonos, muchachos.

(ANDRÉS, PEDRO, ALBERTO *y las dos estudiantes desfilan por la izquierda.*)

ESTUDIANTES	Buenos días. Buenos días, don Pablo.
DON PABLO	Hasta ahora, hijos, hasta ahora.

(*Los estudiantes salen.* ELISA *trata de imitarlos, pero* MIGUELÍN *tira de su brazo y la obliga a sentarse. Con las manos enlazadas vuelven a engolfarse en su charla.* JUANA *y* CARLOS *permanecen de pie, a la izquierda, atendiendo a* DON PABLO. *Breve pausa.*)

THE FATHER	But all these kids are blind, poor things! They see nothing.
MR P.	But they can hear and find their way around better than you. (*The students murmur in agreement.*) In any case… (*Ironically.*) Don't imagine that it's right to refer to them as poor things. Eh, Andy?
ANDY	You've said it.
MR P.	And what do you say, Pete, Al?
PETE	Of course not, we're not poor things.
AL	Anything but.
LINDA	Excuse us, Mr P. …
MR P.	Yes, what is it?
LINDA	(*Amidst laughter.*) Nothing, just that Hope and I think the same.
THE FATHER	Sorry, everyone.
MR P.	We're sorry that this seems like a telling off, when, in fact, it's no more than an explanation. We blind people, or simply, as we say, the non-seers, can get on in life as well as anyone else. We hold down jobs, important posts in journalism and literature, university chairs… We're strong, healthy, sociable… We have a morale of steel. Apart from that, these types of conversations are not what our young people are used to. (*To the others.*) I think that if you were wise, you'd go now and take your places in the main hall. It's almost eleven. (*Smiling.*) That's friendly advice.[12]
ANDY	Thanks, Mr P. Let's go, guys. (ANDY, PETE, AL, LINDA *and* HOPE *file off to the Right.*)
STUDENTS	Good day. Good day, Mr P.
MR P.	I'll be along soon, kids, I'll be along soon. (*The students exit.* LISA *tries to do the same, but* MIKEY *restrains her by the arm, obliging her to sit down. Hand in hand they become engrossed again in their chatting.* JANE *and* CHARLES *remain standing, to the Right, listening to* MR P. *A brief pause.*)

EL PADRE	Estoy avergonzado. Yo...
DON PABLO	No tiene importancia. Usted viene con los prejuicios de las gentes que nos desconocen. Usted, por ejemplo, creerá que nosotros no nos casamos...
EL PADRE	Nada de eso... Entre ustedes, naturalmente...
DON PABLO	No, señor. Los matrimonios entre personas que ven y personas que no ven abundan cada día más. Yo mismo...
EL PADRE	¿Usted?
DON PABLO	Sí. Yo soy invidente de nacimiento y estoy casado con una vidente.
IGNACIO	(*Con lento asombro.*) ¿Una vidente?
EL PADRE	¿Así nos llaman ustedes?
DON PABLO	Sí, señor.
EL PADRE	Perdone, pero... como nosotros llamamos videntes a los que dicen gozar de doble vista...
DON PABLO	(*Algo seco.*) Naturalmente. Pero nosotros, forzosamente más modestos, llamamos así a los que tienen, simplemente, vista.
EL PADRE	(*Que no sabe dónde meterse.*) Dispense una vez más.
DON PABLO	No hay nada que dispensar. Me encantaría presentarle a mi esposa, pero no ha llegado aún. Ignacio la conocerá de todos modos, porque es mi secretaria.
EL PADRE	Otro día será. Bien, Ignacio, hijo... Me marcho contento de dejarte en tan buen lugar. No dudo que te agradará vivir aquí. (*Silencio de* IGNACIO. *A* CARLOS *y* JUANA.) Y ustedes, se lo ruego: ¡levántenle el ánimo! (*Con inhábil jocosidad.*) Infúndanle esa moral de acero que les caracteriza.
IGNACIO	(*Disgustado.*) Padre.
EL PADRE	(*Abrazándole.*) Sí, hijo. De aquí saldrás hecho un hombre...
DON PABLO	Ya lo creo. Todo un señor licenciado, dentro de pocos años.

(*La tensión entre padre e hijo se disuelve.* CARLOS *interviene, tomando del brazo a* IGNACIO.)

THE FATHER	I'm embarrassed. I…
MR P.	Never mind. You've come here with prejudices held by people who don't know us. For example, you'd be thinking that we don't get married…
THE FATHER	No… well… amongst yourselves, of course…
MR P.	No, Sir, no. Marriages between people who can see and those who cannot are becoming more and more frequent. I myself…
THE FATHER	You?
MR P.	Yes. I am a non-seer from birth and I'm married to a seer.[13]
IGGY	(*Slowly, in astonishment.*) A seer?
THE FATHER	Is that what you people call us?
MR P.	Yes, Sir.
THE FATHER	Sorry, but… we call those who have the gift of second sight seers.
MR P.	(*Rather drily.*) Of course, but, having no choice but to be more humble, we use that term for those who simply have sight.
THE FATHER	(*Not knowing which way to turn.*) Sorry… again.
MR P.	There's nothing to be sorry about. I'd love to introduce you to my wife, but she hasn't arrived yet. Iggy will get to know her anyway, because she's my secretary.
THE FATHER	Another time. Ok, Iggy, son… I'm going and I'm happy to leave you in such a fine place. I've no doubt that you'll like living here. (IGGY *stays silent. To* CHARLES *and* JANE.) And the two of you, please, lift his spirits! (*With clumsy jocularity.*) Give him some of that morale of steel that's so much a part of you.
IGGY	(*Annoyed.*) Dad!
THE FATHER	(*Hugging him.*) Yes, son. You'll leave here a man…
MR P.	I believe so. A real gentleman, educated and all, within a few years. (*The tension between father and son dissipates.* CHARLES *moves between them, taking* IGGY *by the hand.*)

CARLOS	Si nos lo permiten, nos llevaremos a nuestro amigo.
EL PADRE	Sí, con mucho gusto. (*Afectado.*) Adiós, Ignacio... Vendré... pronto... a verte.
IGNACIO	(*Indiferente.*) Hasta pronto, padre.

(EL PADRE *está muy afectado; mira a todos con ojos húmedos, que ellos no pueden ver. En sus movimientos muestra múltiples vacilaciones: volver a abrazar a su hijo, despedirse de los dos estudiantes, consultar a* DON PABLO *con una perruna mirada que se pierde en el aire.*)

DON PABLO	¿Vamos?
EL PADRE	Sí, sí.

(*Inician la marcha hacia el foro.*)

DON PABLO	(*Deteniéndose.*) Acompáñele ahora al paraninfo, Carlos. ¡Ah! Y preséntele a Miguelín, porque van a ser compañeros de habitación.
CARLOS	Descuide, don Pablo.

(DON PABLO *acompaña al* PADRE *a la puerta del fondo, por la que salen ambos, mientras le dice una serie de cosas a las que aquél atiende mal, preocupado como está en volverse con frecuencia a ver a su hijo, con una expresión cada vez más acongojada. Al fin, desaparecen tras la cristalera, por la derecha. Entre tanto,* CARLOS, IGNACIO *y* JUANA *se sitúan en el primer término izquierdo.*)

CARLOS	¡Lástima que no vinieses antes! ¿Comienzas ahora la carrera?
IGNACIO	Sí. El preparatorio.
CARLOS	Juana y yo te ayudaremos. No repares en consultarnos cualquier dificultad que encuentres.
JUANA	Desde luego.
CARLOS	Bien. Ahora Miguelín te acomodará en vuestro cuarto. Antes debes aprenderte en seguida el edificio. Escucha: este rincón es nuestra peña, en la que desde ahora quedas admitido. Nada por en medio (*Lo conduce.*), para no tropezar. Le daremos la vuelta, para que aprendas los sillones y veladores. (*Los tres están ahora a la derecha.*) Pero debes abandonar en seguida el bastón. ¡No te hará falta!

CHARLES	If you'll allow us, we'll take our friend off now.
THE FATHER	Yes, with great pleasure. (*Emotionally.*) Goodbye, Iggy... I'll come... soon... to see you.
IGGY	(*Indifferently.*) Whenever, Dad. (*The father is very emotional; he looks at everyone with tear-filled eyes, which they cannot see. In his movements he shows the hesitations besetting him: hugging his son again, taking his leave of the two students, looking to* MR P. *with a hangdog gaze that gets lost in the air.*)
MR P.	Shall we?
THE FATHER	Yes, yes. (*They move off Up-stage.*)
MR P.	(*Stopping.*) Take him to the main hall now, Charles. Ah yes, and introduce him to Mikey, because they're going to be roommates.
CHARLES	No problem, Mr P. (MR P. *accompanies the father to the door Up-stage, through which they both exit, while telling him a series of things to which he does not pay proper heed, concerned as he is about turning around frequently to look at his son, with an expression that is ever more anguished. Finally they disappear behind the French windows, to the Left. Meanwhile* CHARLES, IGGY *and* JANE *occupy Down-stage Right.*)
CHARLES	It's a pity you weren't here before! Are you just starting your studies here now?
IGGY	Yes, in the Foundation Year.
CHARLES	Jane and I'll help you. Don't hesitate to ask us about any problems you might have.
JANE	Yes, of course.
CHARLES	Fine. Mikey will fix you up in your room now. First of all, though, you must learn about the building straight away. Listen, this spot is our club, and you're a member from this very moment. There's nothing in the way (*He leads him around.*), so we don't bump into things. We'll do a little tour, so that you'll learn where the armchairs and tables are. (*The three of them are now on the Left.*) But you've got to give up the stick at once. You'll not need it!

| JUANA | (*Tratando de quitárselo.*) Trae. Se lo daremos al conserje para que lo guarde. |
| IGNACIO | (*Que se resiste.*) No, no. Yo... soy algo torpe para andar sin él. Y no os molestéis tampoco en enseñarme el edificio. No lo aprendería. |

(*Un silencio.*)

CARLOS	Perdona. A tu gusto. Aunque debes intentar vencer rápidamente esa torpeza... ¿No has estudiado en nuestro colegio elemental?
IGNACIO	No.
JUANA	¿No eres de nacimiento?
IGNACIO	Sí. Pero... mi familia...
CARLOS	Bien. No te importe. Todos aquí somos de nacimiento y hemos estudiado en nuestros centros, bajo la dirección de don Pablo.
JUANA	¿Qué te ha parecido don Pablo?
IGNACIO	Un hombre... absurdamente feliz.
CARLOS	Como cualquiera que asistiese a la realización de sus mejores sueños de trabajo. Eso no es un absurdo.
JUANA	Si te oyera doña Pepita...
CARLOS	Ya conocerás a otros profesores no menos dichosos.
IGNACIO	¿Ciegos también?
CARLOS	Se dice invidentes... (*Pausa breve.*) Pues... según. El de Biología es invidente y está casado con la ayudante de Lenguas, que es vidente. También son videntes el de Física, el de...
IGNACIO	Videntes...
JUANA	Videntes. ¿Qué tiene de particular?
IGNACIO	Oye, Carlos, y tú, Juana: ¿acaso es posible el matrimonio entre un ciego y una vidente?
CARLOS	¿Tan raro te parece?
JUANA	¡Si hay muchos!
IGNACIO	¿Y entre un vidente y una ciega? (*Silencio.*) ¿Eh, Carlos? (*Pausa breve.*) ¿Juana?
CARLOS	Juana y yo conocemos uno de viejos...
IGNACIO	Uno.

JANE	(*Trying to get it from him.*) Hand it over. We'll give it to the caretaker for safekeeping.
IGGY	(*Resisting.*) No, no. I... I'm rather clumsy walking without it. And don't bother showing me the building either. I wouldn't learn my way round (*Silence*).
CHARLES	Sorry. As you wish. Although you must try to overcome that clumsiness... Didn't you attend our prep school?
IGGY	No.
JANE	Haven't you been a non-seer from birth?
IGGY	Yes. But... my family...
CHARLES	Ok, it doesn't matter. All of us here are non-seers from birth and we've studied in the different centres under the guidance of Mr P.
JANE	What did you think of Mr P.?
IGGY	He's a man who's... absurdly happy.[14]
CHARLES	Like any man would be, reaching the fulfilment of his finest dreams, regarding his work. That doesn't make him absurd.
JANE	If Mrs P. could hear you now...
CHARLES	You'll soon get to know other teachers who are no less happy.
IGGY	Are they blind too?
CHARLES	We say, 'non-seers'... (*Brief pause.*) Well... it depends. The Biology teacher is a non-seer and he's married to the language assistant, who's a seer. The Physics teacher's a seer too, and so's the...
IGGY	Seers...
JANE	Yes, seers. What's odd about that?
IGGY	Listen, Charles, and Jane: tell me, is marriage between a blind guy and a female seer possible?
CHARLES	Does it seem so strange to you?
JANE	But there are lots!
IGGY	What about between a male seer and a blind girl? (*Silence.*) Eh, Charles? (*Brief pause.*) Jane?
CHARLES	Jane and I know of this old couple...
IGGY	That's one.

JUANA	Y el de Pepe y Luisita. ¡Bien felices son!
IGNACIO	Dos.
CARLOS	(*Sonriendo.*) Ignacio... No te ofendas, pero estás algo afectado por la novedad de encontrarte aquí. ¿Cómo diría yo? Algo... anormal... Serénate. En esta casa sobra alegría para ti y lo pasarás bien.

(*Le da cordiales palmadas en el hombro.* JUANA *sonríe.*)

| IGNACIO | Puede que esté... anormal. Todos lo estamos. |
| CARLOS | (*Sonriendo.*) Ya hablaremos de eso. Aquí hace falta Miguelín, ¿eh, Juana? Me parece que no se ha marchado. ¡Miguelín! (MIGUELÍN *atiende fastidiado, pero sin moverse.*) No te hagas el muerto. Sé que estás aquí. |

(*Tanteando, se dirige a él, que se aprieta contra* ELISA. *Al fin, entre risas, lo toca.*)

MIGUEL	Ya te lo haré yo a ti cuando estés con Juana. ¿Qué pasa?
CARLOS	Ven para acá.
MIGUEL	No me da la gana.
CARLOS	Ven y no hagas el tonto. Tengo que darte una orden de don Pablo.
MIGUEL	(*Incorporándose con desgana.*) Si no se puede considerar incluida Elisita en esa orden, no voy.
ELISA	Podrías dejar de utilizarme para tus chistes, ¿no crees?
MIGUEL	No. No creo.
JUANA	Ven tú también, Elisa. Ya es hora de que estemos juntas algún ratito.
MIGUEL	No hay remedio. (*Suspira.*) En fin, vamos allá. (*Con* ELISA *de su mano, y tras* CARLOS, *se acerca al grupo.*) Desembucha.
CARLOS	(*A* IGNACIO.) Éste es Miguelín: el loco de la casa. El de antes. El rorro de la institución, nuestra mascota de diecisiete años. Así y todo, un gran chico. Elisita es su resignada niñera.
MIGUEL	¡Complaciente! ¡Complaciente niñera!
ELISA	¡Si pudieras callarte!

JANE	And there's Frank and Louise, they're very happy.
IGGY	Two.
CHARLES	(*Smiling.*) Iggy… no offence, but you're a little affected by the novelty of being here, and you're being… how can I put it?… somewhat… abnormal…Relax. In this place there's more than enough happiness to go around and you'll enjoy yourself. (*He gives him a friendly pat on the shoulder.* JANE *smiles.*)
IGGY	I might be, em,… abnormal. We're all like that.
CHARLES	(*Smiling.*) We'll talk about that some other time. We need Mikey here, eh, Jane? I think he hasn't left. Mikey! (*Annoyed, Mikey pays heed, but does not move.*) Don't play dead. I know you're there. (*He gropes his way towards* MIKEY *who squeezes up beside* LISA. *Finally, amidst laughter, he makes contact with him.*)
MIKEY	I'll do that to you sometime when you're with Jane. What's up?
CHARLES	Come here.
MIKEY	I don't want to.
CHARLES	Come here and don't act the fool. I have to give you an order from Mr P.
MIKEY	(*Getting up reluctantly.*) If lovely Lisa isn't part of that order, I'm not coming.
LISA	Could you leave me out of your pranks?
MIKEY	No way.
JANE	Come here, Lisa, you too. It's about time we were together for a little while.
MIKEY	There's no escape. (*He sighs.*) Let's go over. (*Holding* LISA*'s hand, he follows* CHARLES *over to the group.*) Come clean… out with it!
CHARLES	(*To* IGGY.) This is Mikey, the local clown. The guy from earlier on. The big baby, our seventeen-year old mascot. All in all, a great fellow. Lisa is his long-suffering nanny.
MIKEY	Nice nanny, she's a nice nanny!
LISA	Could you be quiet?

MIGUEL	¡Es que no puedo!
CARLOS	Vamos, dad la mano al nuevo.
MIGUEL	(*Haciéndolo, a* ELISA.) Anda..., niñera... Da la mano al nuevo.

(ELISA *lo hace y no puede evitar un ligero estremecimiento.*)

CARLOS	(*A* IGNACIO.) Miguelín será tu compañero de cuarto por disposición superior. Si no congenias con él, dilo y le ajustaremos las cuentas.
IGNACIO	¿Por qué no voy a congeniar? Los dos somos ciegos.

(JUANA *y* ELISA *se emparejan y hablan entre sí.*)

MIGUEL	¿Oyes, Carlos? Cuando yo decía que es un bromista...
IGNACIO	Lo he dicho en serio.
MIGUEL	¡Ah! ¿Sí?... Pues gracias. Aunque yo no me considero muy desgraciado. Mi única desgracia es tener que aguantar a...
ELISA	(*Saltando.*) ¡Calla, estúpido! Ya sé por dónde vas.

(*Todos ríen, menos* IGNACIO.)

MIGUEL	Y mi mayor felicidad, que no hay ninguna suegra preparada.
ELISA	¡Bruto!
MIGUEL	(*A las muchachas.*) ¿Por qué no seguís con vuestros cotilleos? Estabais muy bien así. (*Ellas cuchichean y ríen ahogadamente.*) ¡Las confidencias femeninas, Ignacio! Nada hay más terrible. (JUANA *y* ELISA *le pellizcan.*) ¡Ay! ¡Ay! ¿No lo dije? (*Risas.*) Muy bien. Carlos, Ignacio: propongo una huida en masa hacia la cantina, pero sin las chicas. ¡Hay cerveza!
CARLOS	Aprobado.
JUANA	Frente común, ¿eh? Ya te lo diré luego.
CARLOS	Es un momento...
MIGUEL	¡No capitules, cobarde! Y vámonos de prisa. ¡Damas! El que me corten ustedes a mí lo deseo de raso, con amplios vuelos y tahalí para el espadín. Carlos se conforma con un traje de baño.

MIKEY	I can't.
CHARLES	Come on, shake the new guy's hand.
MIKEY	(*Doing so, he says to* LISA) Come on…, nanny… shake hands with the new arrival. (LISA *does so and cannot help shuddering slightly.*)
CHARLES	(*To* IGGY.) Mikey'll be your roommate… orders from the boss. If you don't get on with him, say so and we'll sort something out.
IGGY	Why wouldn't I get on with him? We're both blind. (JANE *and* LISA *pair off and talk among themselves.*)
MIKEY	Hey, Charles, when I said that he was a funny guy…
IGGY	I mean it, seriously.
MIKEY	Oh, right!… well, thanks. Although I don't consider myself very unfortunate. My only misfortune is that I have to put up with…
LISA	(*Cutting in.*) Quiet, you twit. I know where this is leading. (*Everyone laughs, except for* IGGY.)
MIKEY	And best of all, there's no mother-in-law on the scene.
LISA	You swine!
MIKEY	(*To the girls.*) Why don't you carry on with your gossiping? You were going well. (*They whisper and laugh in a stifled way.*) Secrets among girls, Iggy! There's nothing worse. (JANE *and* LISA *pinch him.*) Ouch, ouch. I didn't say that. (*Laughter.*) Fine. Charles, Iggy: I propose a mass exodus to the canteen, but no girls. There's beer on the go!
CHARLES	Sure thing.
JANE	Team work, eh? I'll have a word with you later.
CHARLES	Shan't be a moment…
MIKEY	Don't give in, you coward. Let's get a move on. Ladies, when you're tearing strips off me, they'll have to be real big ones! But for Charles, a skimpy rag'll do.

JUANA ¡Vete ya!

ELISA (*A la vez.*) ¡Tonto!

(*Con* IGNACIO *en medio, se van los dos muchachos por la derecha.*)

ELISA ¡ Hablemos!

JUANA ¡Hablemos! (*Corren a sentarse, enlazadas, al sofá, en tanto que* DON PABLO *cruza tras los cristales y entra por la puerta del foro. Se acerca a las muchachas, escucha y se detiene a su lado.*) ¡Cuánto tiempo sin decirnos cosas!

ELISA Lo necesitaba como el pan.

DON PABLO ¿Tal vez interrumpo?

JUANA Nada de eso. (*Se levantan las dos.*) Casi no habíamos empezado.

DON PABLO ¿Y de qué iban a hablar? ¿Acaso del nuevo alumno?

ELISA A mí me parece... que íbamos a hablar de alumnos más antiguos.

JUANA (*Avergonzada.*) ¡Elisa!

DON PABLO (*Riendo.*) Una conversación muy agradable. (*Serio.*) Pero ha venido este viejo importuno y prefiere hablar del alumno nuevo. Supongo que Elisita ya lo conoce.

ELISA Sí, señor.

(*Por la terraza ha cruzado* DOÑA PEPITA, *que se detiene en la puerta. Cuarenta años. Trae una cartera de cuero bajo el brazo. Sonriente, contempla con cariño a su esposo.*)

DON PABLO (*Que la percibe inmediatamente y vuelve su mirada al vacío.*) Un momento... Mi mujer...

(*Termina de volverse.*)

DOÑA PEPITA (*Acercándose.*) Hola, Pablo. Dispénsame; ya sé que vengo algo retrasada.

DON PABLO (*Tomándole una mano, con una ternura que los años no parecen haber aminorado.*) Hueles muy bien hoy, Pepita.

DOÑA PEPITA Igual que siempre. Buenos días, señoritas. ¿Dónde dejaron a sus caballeros andantes?

JANE	Go on with you!
LISA	(*Simultaneously.*) You fool! (*With* IGGY *in between them, the two boys move to the Left.*)
LISA	Let's talk.
JANE	Yeah, let's talk. (*They run to sit down, arm in arm, on the sofa, as* MR P. *passes behind the windows and enters by the door Up-stage. He goes over to the girls, listens and stops beside them.*) We haven't talked in ages!
LISA	I really need this.
MR P.	Am I intruding?
JANE	Not at all. (*The two girls get up.*) We had hardly started.
MR P.	And what were you going to talk about; the new student, perhaps?
LISA	I think that... we were going to talk about students who've been here rather longer.
JANE	(*Embarrassed.*) Lisa!
MR P.	(*Laughing.*) Now that would be a nice chat. (*Seriously.*) But this awkward old chap has come along and prefers to talk about the new student. I guess our little Lisa knows him already.
LISA	Yes, Sir. (MRS P., *who has come across the terrace, stops at the door. She is around forty years of age. She carries a leather briefcase under her arm. Smiling, she gazes affectionately at her husband.*)
MR P.	(*Who is immediately aware of her and turns to stare blankly.*) Just a moment... my wife. (*He completes his about-turn.*)
MRS P.	(*Approaching.*) Hello, Paul. Excuse me, I know I'm rather late.
MR P.	(*Taking her by the hand with an affection which the years do not seem to have diminished.*) You smell really lovely today, Fran.
MRS P.	Same as always. Good day, girls. Where did you leave your knights in shining armour?

ELISA	Nos abandonaron por un nuevo amigote.
JUANA	Pobre chico. Es simpático.
ELISA	A mí no me lo es.
DON PABLO	No hable así de un compañero, señorita. Y menos cuando aún no ha tenido tiempo de conocerlo. (*A* DOÑA PEPITA.) Carlos y Miguelín están acompañando a un alumno nuevo del preparatorio que acaban de traernos.
DOÑA PEPITA	¿Ah, sí? ¿Qué tal chico es?
DON PABLO	Ya has oído que a estas señoritas no les merece una opinión muy favorable.
JUANA	¿Por qué no? Es que Elisa es muy precipitada.
DON PABLO	Sí, un poco. Y, por eso mismo, les haré a las dos algunas recomendaciones.
JUANA	¿Respecto a Ignacio?
DON PABLO	Sí. (*A* DOÑA PEPITA.) Y, de paso, también tú te harás cargo de la cuestión.
DOÑA PEPITA	¿Es algo grave?
DON PABLO	Es lo de siempre. Falta de moral.
DOÑA PEPITA	El caso típico.
DON PABLO	Típico. Quizás un poquitín complicado esta vez. Un muchacho triste, malogrado por el mal entendido amor de los padres. Mucho mimo, profesores particulares... Hijo único. En fin, ya lo comprendes. Es preciso, como en otras ocasiones, la ayuda inteligente de algunos estudiantes.
JUANA	Intentamos antes que abandonara el bastón y no quiso. Dice que es muy torpe.
DON PABLO	Pues hay que convencerle de que es un ser útil y de que tiene abiertos todos los caminos, si se atreve. Es cierto que aquí tiene el ejemplo, pero hay que administrárselo con tacto, y al talento de ustedes, señoritas. (*A* JUANA.), y al de Carlos, muy particularmente, recomiendo la parte más importante: la creación de una camaradería verdadera que le alegre el corazón. No les será muy difícil... Los muchachos de este tipo están hambrientos de cariño y alegría y no suelen rechazarlos cuando se saben romper sus murallas interiores.

LISA   They dumped us for a new little friend.

JANE   Poor boy. He's nice.

LISA   I don't think he is.

MR P.   Don't speak like that of a fellow student, young lady. Especially when you haven't really yet had time to get to know him. (*To* MRS P.) Charles and Mikey are off with a new student from the Foundation Year who's just been brought to us.

MRS P.   Oh, yes, and what kind of chap is he?

MR P.   Well, you've heard that these young ladies don't rate him very highly.

JANE   I wouldn't go that far. Lisa's too quick to criticise.

MR P.   She is, rather. And that's why I'll give the two of you some advice.

JANE   With regard to Iggy?

MR P.   Yes. (*To* MRS P.) Oh, yes, and, by the way, you'll now also be in on this.

MRS P.   Is it something serious?

MR P.   The usual thing. Lack of morale.

MRS P.   The typical case.

MR P.   Typical, yes. Perhaps a little complicated in this instance. He's a sad young fellow, stymied by misguided love from his parents. A lot of pampering, private tutors... an only child. All in all, you get the picture. As on other occasions, meaningful help from certain students is needed.

JANE   We tried earlier to get him to give up his stick, but he didn't want to. He says he's very clumsy.

MR P.   Well, look, we just have to convince him that he's a useful being and that all roads are open to him, if he takes a chance. Here he certainly has the example to follow, but it's got to be put to him tactfully, and to your special talents, ladies (*To* JANE.) and to those of Charles, in particular, I entrust the most important task: that of creating a real sense of camaraderie that will lift his spirits. It won't be difficult for you... Boys of that type are hungry for affection and happiness and they don't usually reject those things when people know how to break down their inner barriers.[15]

DOÑA PEPITA	¿Por qué no lo pones de compañero de habitación con Miguelín?
DON PABLO	(*Asintiendo, sonriente.*) Ya está hecho... Pero no es preciso, señorita Elisa, que Miguelín sea informado de esta recomendación mía. Si lo tomase como un encargo, le saldría mal.
ELISA	No le diré nada.
DOÑA PEPITA	Bueno. La cuestión se reduce a impregnar a ese Ignacio, en el plazo más breve, de nuestra famosa moral de acero. ¿No es así?
DON PABLO	Exacto. Y basta de charla, que el acto de la apertura se aproxima. Señoritas: en ustedes... cuatro descanso satisfecho para este asunto.
JUANA	Descuide, don Pablo.
DOÑA PEPITA	Hasta ahora, hijitas.
JUANA	Hasta ahora, doña Pepita.
DOÑA PEPITA	Pablo, si no dispones otra cosa, mandaré conectar los altavoces. Los chicos tienen derecho a su ratito de música hasta la apertura...

(*Se van charlando por la izquierda.* JUANA *y* ELISA *se pasean torpemente en primer término, en cariñoso emparejamiento.*)

JUANA	¡Hablemos! (ELISA *no contesta. Parece preocupada.* JUANA *insiste.*) ¡Hablemos, Elisa!
ELISA	(*Cavilosa.*) No me agrada el encargo del director. Ese Ignacio tiene algo indefinible que me repele. ¿Tú crees en el fluido magnético?
JUANA	Sí, mujer. ¿Quién de nosotros no?
ELISA	Muchos aseguran que eso es falso.
JUANA	Muchos tontos... que no están enamorados.
ELISA	(*Riendo.*) Tienes razón. Pero ése es el fluido bueno, y tiene que haber otro malo.
JUANA	¿Cuál?
ELISA	(*Grave.*) El de Ignacio. Cuando estaba con nosotras me pareció percibir una sensación de ahogo, una desazón y una molestia... Y cuando le di la mano se acentuó terriblemente. Una mano seca, ardorosa... ¡Cargada de malas intenciones!

MRS P.	Why don't you room him with Mikey?
MR P.	(*Nodding and smiling.*) That's been arranged… but, Miss Lisa, there's no need to tell Mikey about my plan. If it comes as an order, he wouldn't like it.
LISA	I'll say nothing to him.
MRS P.	Well, then, the whole thing boils down to imbuing this Iggy character, as quickly as possible, with our famous morale of steel. Isn't that the idea?
MR P.	That's it. That's enough talk for now, the opening assembly is about to start. Ladies,… I'll leave this case to rest in your hands, the four of you.
JANE	No problem, Mr P.
MRS P.	See you in a moment, girls.
JANE	Ok, Mrs P.
MRS P.	Paul, if there's nothing else, I'll have the loudspeakers connected up. The kids are entitled to their little spot of music until the ceremony begins. (*They head off to the Right chatting.* JANE *and* LISA *move clumsily Downstage, pairing off affectionately.*)
JANE	Let's talk. (LISA *doesn't answer. She seems preoccupied.* JANE *insists.*) Let's talk, Lisa!
LISA	(*Pondering.*) I don't like the boss's orders. That Iggy guy has something strange about him that repels me. Do you believe in personal magnetism?
JANE	Yes, of course. Who amongst us doesn't?
LISA	Lots of people say it's not true.
JANE	A bunch of fools… who aren't in love.
LISA	(*Laughing.*) You're right. But that's the good sort of magnetism; there's got to be another, bad sort.
JANE	Oh yeah, what's that?
LISA	(*Gravely.*) The sort Iggy gives off. When he was with us I seemed to feel a sense of suffocation, unease, botheration… and when I shook hands with him, it got much worse. He has a dry, feverish hand… full of evil intent!

JUANA	Yo no noté eso. A mí me pareció simpático. (*Breve pausa.*) Y, sobre todo, es un ser desgraciado. Ese chico necesita adaptarse, nada más. ¡Y no pienses en esas tonterías del fluido maligno!
ELISA	(*Maliciosa.*) ¡Pues prefiero el fluido de Miguelín!
JUANA	(*Riendo.*) ¡Y yo el de Carlos! Pero calla. Se me ocurre una cosa...

(*Silencio. De pronto comienzan los altavoces lejanos a desgranar en el ambiente el adagio del «Claro de luna», de Beethoven, lentamente tocado.*)

| ELISA | ¿Eh? |
| JUANA | Escucha. ¡Qué hermoso! |

(*Pausa.*)

ELISA	Podemos seguir hablando, ¿no te parece?
JUANA	Sí, sí. Te dije que callaras porque había encontrado... la solución del problema de Ignacio.
ELISA	¿Sí? ¡Dime!
JUANA	(*Con dulzura.*) La solución para Ignacio es... una novia... Y tenemos que encontrársela. Pensaremos juntas en todas nuestras amigas. (*Pausa breve.*) ¿No me dices nada? ¿No lo encuentras bien?
ELISA	Sí, pero...
JUANA	¡Es una idea magnífica! ¿Ya no te acuerdas de cuando paseábamos juntas, antes de que Carlos y Miguelín se decidiesen? No negarás que entonces estábamos bastante tristes... No habíamos llegado aún a la región de la alegría, como dice Carlos. (ELISA *la besa.*) ¡Y qué emoción cuando cambiamos las primeras confidencias! Cuando te dije: «¡Se me ha declarado, Elisa!».
ELISA	Y yo te pregunté: «¿Cómo ha sido? ¡Anda, cuéntamelo!».
JUANA	Sí. Y también, a una pregunta mía, me dijiste, melancólicamente: «No... Miguelín aún no me ha dicho nada... No me quiere».
ELISA	¡Y lo hizo al día siguiente!

JANE	I didn't get that sense. To me, he seemed nice. (*Brief pause.*) And, above all, he's an unhappy soul. That guy needs to fit in, that's all. And forget about that silly personal magnetism.
LISA	(*Mischievously.*) Well, anyway, I prefer Mikey's variety!
JANE	(*Laughing.*) And Charles's for me! But, shush, I have an idea… (*Silence. Suddenly the distant loudspeakers begin to emit the gentle strains of the adagio from Beethoven's 'Moonlight Sonata'.*)
LISA	What's that?
JANE	Listen. How lovely! (*A pause.*)
LISA	We can carry on talking, can't we?
JANE	Yeah, yeah. I told you to be quiet because I had found… the solution to the Iggy problem.
LISA	Really?
JANE	(*Sweetly.*) The solution for Iggy is… a girlfriend… And we've got to find her for him. We'll both think of all our female friends. (*Brief pause.*) Has the cat got your tongue? Don't you like the idea?
LISA	Yes, but…
JANE	It's a great idea! Don't you remember the times when we used to hang out together, before Charles and Mikey committed themselves to us? You wouldn't deny that we were pretty sad in those days… We hadn't reached the happiness zone, as Charles puts it. (LISA *gives her a kiss.*) And the feeling when we first told each other the news! When I said to you: 'He's asked me out, Lisa!'[16]
LISA	And I asked you: 'How was it? Go on, tell me!'
JANE	Yes. And also, when you replied to one of my questions with a big sad face: 'No… Mikey still hasn't said anything to me… He doesn't love me.'
LISA	And he asked me the next day!

JUANA	Animado, sin duda, por el mío. Son unos granujas. Ellos también tienen sus confidencias.
ELISA	Y después..., el primer beso...
JUANA	(*Soñadora.*) O antes...
ELISA	(*Estupefacta.*) ¿Qué?

(*Pero se asusta repentinamente ante las llamadas de* MIGUELÍN, *en las que palpita un tono de angustia.*)

MIGUEL	¡Elisa! ¡Elisa! ¡Elisa!

(*Aparece por la derecha.*)

ELISA	(*Corriendo hacia él asustada.*) ¡Aquí estoy, Miguelín! ¿Por qué gritas?
MIGUEL	¡Ven!... (*Cambiando súbitamente el tono por uno de broma.*) que te abrace.

(*Llega y lo hace, entre las risas de su novia.*)

ELISA	¡Pegajoso!
JUANA	Hay moros en la costa, Miguelín.
MIGUEL	Ya, ya lo sé. Sacándonos a los cristianos el pellejo a tiras. Pero se acabó. Vámonos, Elisa.
JUANA	¿Y Carlos?
MIGUEL	No tardará. Me ha dicho que le esperes aquí.
JUANA	¿Dónde habéis dejado a Ignacio?
MIGUEL	En mi cuarto ha quedado. Dice que está cansado y que no asistirá a la apertura... Bueno, Elisita, que hay que coger buen sitio.
ELISA	Sí, vámonos. ¿Te quedas, Juana?
JUANA	Ahora vamos Carlos y yo... Guardadnos sitio.
MIGUEL	Se procurará. Hasta ahora.

(ELISA *y* MIGUELÍN *se van por la izquierda.* JUANA *queda sola. Pasea lentamente, mientras escucha la sonata. Suspira. Un nuevo ruido interviene repentinamente: el inconfundible «tap-tap» de un bastón.* JUANA *se inmoviliza y escucha. Por la derecha aparece* IGNACIO, *que se dirige, despacio, al foro.*)

JUANA	¡Ignacio! (IGNACIO *se detiene.*) Eres Ignacio, ¿no?
IGNACIO	Sí, soy Ignacio. Y tú eres Juana.

JANE	No doubt spurred on by my man. They're rascals. They've got their secrets too.
LISA	And then afterwards… the first kiss…
JANE	(*Dreamily.*) Or was it before?
LISA	(*Astonished.*) What? (*But suddenly she is frightened by* MIKEY*'s cries, in which a note of anguish rings out.*)
MIKEY	Lisa, Lisa, Lisa! (*He appears to the Left.*)
LISA	(*Running towards him, frightened.*) Here I am, Mikey! Why are you shouting?
MIKEY	Come here!… (*Quickly changing his tone to a humorous one.*)… and I'll hug you. (*He reaches her and hugs her, amidst laughter from his girlfriend.*)
LISA	You big sop!
JANE	Walls have ears, Mikey.
MIKEY	Yeah, yeah, I know. Some people have got it in for us. That's it, now. Let's go, Lisa.
JANE	What about Charles?
MIKEY	He won't be long. He says you're to wait here for him.
JANE	Where did you leave Iggy?
MIKEY	He's stayed in my room. He says he's tired and won't attend the opening assembly… Ok, Lisa, honey, we'd better get a good seat.
LISA	Yeah, let's go. Are you staying, Jane?
JANE	Charles and I'll be along… keep us a place.
MIKEY	We'll try. See you soon. (LISA *and* MIKEY *head off to the Right.* JANE *is alone. She walks about slowly, while listening to the sonata. She sighs. A new sound is suddenly heard: the unmistakable 'tap-tap' of a stick.* JANE *stops and listens. To the Right appears* IGGY *who moves slowly Up-stage.*)
JANE	Iggy! (IGGY *stops.*) It's Iggy isn't it?
IGGY	Yes, it's Iggy. And you're Jane.

JUANA	(*Acercándose.*) ¿No estabas en tu cuarto?
IGNACIO	De allí vengo... Adiós.

(*Comienza a andar.*)

JUANA	¿Dónde vas?
IGNACIO	(*Frío.*) A mi casa. (JUANA *se queda muda de asombro.*) Adiós.

(*Da unos pasos.*)

JUANA	Pero Ignacio... ¡Si ibas a estudiar con nosotros!
IGNACIO	(*Deteniéndose.*) He cambiado de parecer.
JUANA	¿En una hora?
IGNACIO	Es suficiente.

(JUANA *se acerca y le coge cariñosamente de las solapas. Él se inmuta.*)

JUANA	No te dejes llevar de ese impulso irrazonable... ¿Cómo vas a llegar a tu casa?
IGNACIO	(*Nervioso, rehuyendo torpemente el contacto de ella.*) Eso es fácil.
JUANA	¡Pero tu padre se llevará un disgusto grandísimo! ¿Y qué dirá don Pablo?
IGNACIO	(*Despectivo.*) Don Pablo...
JUANA	Y nosotros, todos nosotros lo sentiríamos. Te consideramos ya como un compañero... Un buen compañero, con quien pasar alegremente un curso inolvidable.
IGNACIO	¡Calla! Todos tenéis el acierto de crisparme. ¡Y tú también! ¡Tú la primera! «Alegremente» es la palabra de la casa. Estáis envenenados de alegría. Y no era eso lo que pensaba yo encontrar aquí. Creí que encontraría... a mis verdaderos compañeros, no a unos ilusos.
JUANA	(*Sonriendo con dulzura.*) Pobre Ignacio, me das pena.
IGNACIO	¡Guárdate tu pena!
JUANA	¡No te enfades! Es muy natural lo que te pasa. Todos hemos vivido momentos semejantes, pero eso concluye un día. (*Ladina.*) Y yo sé el remedio. (*Breve pausa.*) Si me escuchas con tranquilidad, te diré cuál es.
IGNACIO	¡Estoy tranquilo!
JUANA	Óyeme... Tú necesitas una novia. (*Pausa.* IGNACIO

JANE	(*Coming nearer.*) Weren't you in your room?
IGGY	I've just come from there… Goodbye. (*He starts to walk off.*)
JANE	Where are you going?
IGGY	(*Coldly.*) Home. (JANE *is left speechless with astonishment.*) Goodbye. (*He takes a few steps.*)
JANE	But Iggy… you were going to study with us.
IGGY	(*Stopping.*) I've changed my mind.
JANE	In the space of an hour?
IGGY	It's time enough. (JANE *approaches him and takes him tenderly by the lapels. He becomes worried.*)
JANE	Don't act on this irrational impulse… How are you going to get home?
IGGY	(*Nervous, clumsily shying away from contact with her.*) That's easy.
JANE	But your father'll be really annoyed! And what'll Mr P. say?
IGGY	(*Contemptuously.*) Mr P. …
JANE	And us, we'd all be sorry. We already think of you as one of us… You're a good fellow student. We could happily spend an unforgettable year with you.
IGGY	Stop it! You're all determined to get on my nerves. You, as well! You're the worst of all! 'Happily' seems to be the key word around here. You're all poisoned with happiness.[17] And that wasn't what I expected to find here. I thought I'd find… true companions, not a bunch of dreamers.
JANE	(*Smiling sweetly.*) Poor Iggy. I pity you.
IGGY	Keep your pity to yourself!
JANE	Don't get angry! What's happening to you is very normal. We've all lived through similar situations, but all that stops one day. (*Slyly.*) And I know the answer. (*Brief pause.*) If you listen calmly, I'll tell you.
IGGY	I *am* calm!
JANE	Listen to me… you need a girlfriend. (*Pause.* IGGY *starts*

comienza a reír levemente.) ¡Te ríes! (*Risueña.*) ¡Pronto acerté!

IGNACIO   (*Deja de reír. Grave.*) Estáis envenenados de alegría. Pero sois monótonos y tristes sin saberlo... Sobre todo las mujeres. Aquí, como ahí fuera, os repetís lamentablemente, seáis ciegas o no. No eres la primera en sugerirme esa solución pueril. Mis vecinitas decían lo mismo.

JUANA   ¡Bobo! ¿No comprendes que se insinuaban?

IGNACIO   ¡No! Ellas también estaban comprometidas..., como tú. Daban el consejo estúpido que la estúpida alegría amorosa os pone a todas en la boca. Es... como una falsa generosidad. Todas decís: «¿Por qué no te echas novia?». Pero ninguna, con la inefable emoción del amor en la voz, ha dicho: «Te quiero». (*Furioso.*) Ni tú tampoco, ¿no es así? ¿O acaso lo dices? (*Pausa.*) No necesito una novia. ¡Necesito un «te quiero» dicho con toda el alma! «Te quiero con tu tristeza y tu angustia; para sufrir contigo, y no para llevarte a ningún falso reino de la alegría». No hay mujeres así.

JUANA   (*Vagamente dolida en su condición femenina.*) Acaso tú no le hayas preguntado a ninguna mujer.

IGNACIO   (*Duro.*) ¿A una vidente?

JUANA   ¿Por qué no?

IGNACIO   (*Irónico.*) ¿A una vidente?

JUANA   ¡Qué mas da! ¡A una mujer!

(*Breve pausa.*)

IGNACIO   ¡Al diablo todas, y tú de capitana! Quédate con tu alegría; con tu Carlos, muy bueno y muy sabio... y completamente tonto, porque se cree alegre. Y como él, Miguelín, y don Pablo y todos. ¡Todos! Que no tenéis derecho a vivir, porque os empeñáis en no sufrir; porque os negáis a enfrentaros con vuestra tragedia, fingiendo una normalidad que no existe, procurando olvidar e, incluso, aconsejando duchas de alegría para reanimar a los tristes... (*Movimiento de* JUANA.) ¡Crees que no lo sé!

	laughing slightly.) You can laugh all you like! (*She smiles.*) I think I hit the nail on the head just now!
IGGY	(*Stops laughing. Seriously.*) You're all poisoned with happiness. But you're monotonous and sad, without being aware of it... Especially the women. Here, like out there, you're all the same, blind or not. You're not the first female to suggest that childish solution to me. The girls round where I live used to say the same thing.
JANE	Silly you! Don't you understand what they were getting at?
IGGY	No! They had steady boyfriends too... like you. They were giving out the sort of stupid advice which stupid lovey-dovey happiness makes you all come out with. It's... like false generosity. You all say: 'Why don't you get yourself a girlfriend?' But not one of you, with the indescribable feeling of love in your voice, has said: 'I love you.' (*In a fury.*) You're no different, are you? Or perhaps you do say that? (*Pause.*) I don't need a girlfriend. I need to hear 'I love you' said with feeling! 'I love you with your sadness and anguish; to suffer with you and not to carry you off to any false kingdom of happiness.' There aren't any women like that.[18]
JANE	(*Vaguely wounded as a woman.*) Perhaps you've never asked any woman.
IGGY	(*Tough.*) What about asking a female seer?
JANE	Why not?
IGGY	(*Sarcastically.*) A female seer?
JANE	What does it matter? A woman, for God's sake! (*Brief pause.*)
IGGY	To hell with all you women, and you, especially! You can keep your happiness; your very good and very wise Charles... who's completely stupid, because he thinks he's happy. And along with him, Mikey, Mr P. and the lot of you. The whole gang! You don't have the right to live, because you are determined not to suffer; because you refuse to confront your tragedy, feigning a non-existent normality, trying to forget and even prescribing the happiness treatment to cheer up the sad cases... (JANE *moves.*) Do you think I don't know? I've guessed it. Your

Lo adivino. Tu don Pablo tuvo la candidez de insinuárselo a mi padre, y éste os lo pidió descaradamente... (*Sarcástico.*) Vosotros sois los alumnos modelo, los leales colaboradores del profesorado en la lucha contra la desesperación, que se agazapa por todos los rincones de la casa. (*Pausa.*) ¡Ciegos! ¡Ciegos y no invidentes, imbéciles!

JUANA   (*Conmovida.*) No sé qué decirte... Ni quiero mentirte tampoco... Pero respeta y agradece al menos nuestro buen deseo. ¡Quédate! Prueba...

IGNACIO   No.

JUANA   ¡Por favor! No puedes marcharte ahora; sería escandaloso. Y yo... No acierto con las palabras. No sé cómo podría convencerte.

IGNACIO   No puedes convencerme.

JUANA   (*Con las manos juntas, alterada.*) No te vayas. Soy muy torpe, lo comprendo... Tú aciertas a darme la sensación de mi impotencia... Si te vas, todos sabrán que hablé contigo y no conseguí nada. ¡Quédate!

IGNACIO   ¡Vanidosa!

JUANA   (*Condolida.*) No es vanidad, Ignacio. (*Triste.*) ¿Quieres que te lo pida de rodillas?

(*Breve pausa.*)

IGNACIO   (*Muy frío.*) ¿Para qué de rodillas? Dicen que ese gesto causa mucha impresión a los videntes... Pero nosotros no lo vemos. No seas tonta; no hables de cosas que desconoces, no imites a los que viven de verdad. ¡Y ahórrame tu desagradable debilidad, por favor! (*Gran pausa.*) Me quedo.

JUANA   ¡Gracias!

IGNACIO   ¿Gracias? Hacéis mal negocio. Porque vosotros sois demasiado pacíficos, demasiado insinceros, demasiado fríos. Pero yo estoy ardiendo por dentro; ardiendo con un fuego terrible, que no me deja vivir y que puede haceros arder a todos... Ardiendo en esto que los videntes llaman oscuridad, y que es horroroso..., porque no sabemos lo que es. Yo os voy a traer guerra y no paz.

	Mr P. was naïve enough to hint as much to my father, and he brazenly asked you to do it... (*Sarcastically.*) Your crowd are the model students, faithful collaborators with the teaching staff in the struggle against despair, which lurks in every corner in this place. (*Pause.*) You are blind! Blind, not non-seers, you fools![19]
JANE	(*Moved.*) I don't know what to say to you... nor do I want to lie to you... but, at least, respect and appreciate our good intentions. Stay. Try...
IGGY	No!
JANE	Please! You can't leave now; it'd be awful. And I... I'm no good with words. I don't know how I'd be able to convince you.
IGGY	You can't convince me.
JANE	(*With her hands joined, and affected by it all.*) Don't go. I know I'm awkward... you've managed to give me the feeling of my own helplessness... If you go they'll all know that I spoke to you and achieved nothing. Stay!
IGGY	You're so vain!
JANE	(*Hurt.*) It isn't vanity, Iggy. (*Sadly.*) Do you want me to beg on my knees? (*Brief pause.*)
IGGY	(*Very coldly.*) Why get on your knees? They say that has a big effect on seers... but we can't see it. Don't be foolish; don't talk about things you don't know; don't copy those who live real lives. And spare me that pathetic show of weakness, please! (*Long pause.*) I'll stay.
JANE	Thank you!
IGGY	Thanks, is it? You're all getting a bad deal. Because you're all too peace-loving, too insincere, too cold. But me, I'm burning up inside, burning with a terrible fire, which doesn't let me live and can burn you all up... I'm burning in what the seers call darkness, which is horrifying..., because we don't know what it is. I'll bring you war, not peace.

JUANA	No hables así. Me duele. Lo esencial es que te quedes. Estoy segura de que será bueno para todos.
IGNACIO	(*Burlón.*) Torpe... y tonta. Tu optimismo y tu ceguera son iguales... La guerra que me consume os consumirá.
JUANA	(*Nuevamente afligida.*) No, Ignacio. No debes traernos ninguna guerra. ¿No será posible que todos vivamos en paz? No te comprendo bien. ¿Por qué sufres tanto? ¿Qué te pasa? ¿Qué es lo que quieres?

(*Breve pausa.*)

IGNACIO	(*Con tremenda energía contenida.*) ¡Ver!
JUANA	(*Se separa de él y queda sobrecogida.*) ¿Qué?
IGNACIO	¡Sí! ¡Ver! Aunque sé que es imposible, ¡ver! Aunque en este deseo se consuma estérilmente mi vida entera, ¡quiero ver! No puedo conformarme. No debemos conformarnos. ¡Y menos, sonreír! Y resignarse con vuestra estúpida alegría de ciegos, ¡nunca! (*Pausa.*) Y aunque no haya ninguna mujer de corazón que sea capaz de acompañarme en mi calvario, marcharé solo, negándome a vivir resignado, ¡porque quiero ver!

(*Pausa. Los altavoces lejanos siguen sonando.* JUANA *está paralizada, con la mano en la boca y la angustia en el semblante.* CARLOS *irrumpe rápido por la derecha.*)

CARLOS	¡Juana! (*Silencio.* JUANA *se vuelve hacia él, instintivamente; luego, desconcertada, se vuelve a* IGNACIO, *sin decidirse a hablar.*) ¿No estás aquí, Juanita?... ¡Juana! (JUANA *no se mueve ni contesta.* IGNACIO, *sumido en su amargura, tampoco.* CARLOS *pierde su instintiva seguridad; se siente extrañamente solo. Ciego. Adelanta indeciso los brazos, en el gesto eterno de palpar el aire, y avanza con precaución.*) ¡Juana!... ¡Juana!...

(*Sale por la izquierda llamándola, de nuevo con voz segura y trivial*)

TELÓN

JANE   Don't talk like that. It hurts me. The important thing is that you're staying. I'm sure that'll be good for everyone.

IGGY   (*Mockingly.*) You're a little slow on it... and foolish. Your optimism and your blindness are the same... The war that's consuming me will devour you all.

JANE   (*Upset again.*) No, Iggy. You mustn't bring us war. Won't it be possible for all of us to live in peace? I don't really understand you. Why do you suffer so? What's happening to you? What do you want? (*Brief pause.*)

IGGY   (*With tremendous pent-up energy.*) To see!

JANE   (*Moves away from him, deeply affected.*) What?

IGGY   Yes! To see! Though I know it's impossible, to see! Though my whole life is wasted in that desire, I want to see! I can't accept things as they are! We mustn't accept things as they are. And we certainly shouldn't smile in the face of it! And resigning yourself to it with that stupid blind happiness, never! (*Pause.*) And even if there is no true-hearted woman capable of accompanying me in my living hell, I'll go on alone, refusing to live in resignation. Because I want to see! (*Pause. The distant loudspeakers continue to sound out.* JANE *stands transfixed, her hand to her mouth and anguish on her face.* CHARLES *bursts in on the Left.*)[20]

CHARLES   Jane! (*Silence.* JANE *turns around towards him, instinctively; then, disconcertedly, she turns towards* IGGY, *unsure whether or not to speak.*) Jane, are you here?... Janey! (JANE *neither moves nor answers.* IGGY, *overwhelmed by his own bitterness, does likewise.* CHARLES *loses his instinctive certainty, he feels strangely alone. Blind. Indecisively he puts his arms out in front of him, with the eternal gesture of feeling the air, and moves cautiously forward.*) Jane!... Jane!...

(*He exits Right calling her, with the light, assured tone restored to his voice.*)[21]

CURTAIN

ACTO SEGUNDO

El fumadero. Los árboles del fondo muestran ahora el esqueleto de sus ramas, sólo aquí y allá moteadas de hojas amarillas. En el suelo de la terraza abundan las hojas secas, que el viento trae y lleva.

(ELISA *se encuentra en la terraza, recostada en el quicio de la portalada, con el aire mustio y los cabellos alborotados por la brisa. Después de un momento, entran por la derecha* JUANA *y* CARLOS, *del brazo. En vano intentan ocultarse el uno al otro su tono preocupado.*)

CARLOS   Juana...
JUANA   Dime.
CARLOS   ¿Qué te ocurre?
JUANA   Nada.
CARLOS   No intentes negármelo. Llevas ya algún tiempo así...
JUANA   (*Con falsa ligereza.*) ¿Así, cómo?
CARLOS   Así como... inquieta.

(*Se sienta en uno de los sillones del centro.* JUANA *lo hace en el sofá, a su lado.*)

JUANA   No es nada...

(*Breve pausa.*)

CARLOS   Siempre nos dijimos nuestras preocupaciones... ¿No quieres darme el placer de compartir ahora las tuyas?
JUANA   ¡Si no estoy preocupada!

(*Breve pausa.*)

CARLOS   (*Acariciándole una mano.*) Sí. Sí lo estás. Y yo también.
JUANA   ¿Tú? ¿Tú estás preocupado? Pero ¿por qué?
CARLOS   Por la situación que ha creado... Ignacio.

(*Breve pausa.*)

JUANA   ¿La crees grave?
CARLOS   ¿Y tú? (*Sonriendo.*) Vamos, sincérate conmigo... Siempre lo hiciste.

ACT II

The students' common room. Now the branches on the trees Up-stage are virtually bare, with only the odd yellow leaf speckled here and there. The terrace is covered by dry leaves blown about by the wind.

(LISA *is on the terrace, leaning at the door, rather down in the mouth, her hair ruffled by the breeze. After a moment,* JANE *and* CHARLES *enter Left, arm-in-arm. They vainly try to hide from each other the worried timbre in their voices.*)[22]

CHARLES	Jane...
JANE	Yes.
CHARLES	What's up with you?
JANE	Nothing.
CHARLES	Don't give me that. You've been like this for some time...
JANE	(*Pretending to make light of things.*) Like what?
CHARLES	Sort of... anxious. (*He sits in one of the armchairs Centre-stage.* JANE *sits on the nearby sofa.*)
JANE	It's nothing... (*Brief pause.*)
CHARLES	We've always told each other our problems. Don't you want to share yours with me now?
JANE	But, honestly, I'm not worried. (*Brief pause.*)
CHARLES	(*Stroking her hand.*) Yes, you are. And I am too.
JANE	You? You're worried? But, why?
CHARLES	Because of the situation created by... Iggy. (*Brief pause.*)
JANE	Do you think it's serious?
CHARLES	Do you? (*Smiling.*) Come on, be straight with me... like you always were.

JUANA	No sé qué pensar... Me considero parcialmente culpable.
CARLOS	(*Sin entonación.*) ¿Culpable?
JUANA	Sí. Ya te dije que el día de la apertura logré disuadirle de su propósito de marcharse. Y ahora pienso que quizá hubiera sido mejor.
CARLOS	Hubiera sido mejor; pero todavía es posible arreglar las cosas, ¿no crees?
JUANA	Tal vez.
CARLOS	Ayer tuve que decirle lo mismo a don Pablo... Es sorprendente lo afectado que está. No supo concretarme nada; pero se desahogó confiándome sus aprensiones... Encuentra a los muchachos más reservados, menos decididos que antes. Los concursos de emulación en el estudio se realizan ahora mucho más lánguidamente... Yo traté de animarle. Me causaba lástima encontrarle tan indeciso. Lástima... y una sensación muy rara.
JUANA	¿Una sensación muy rara? ¿Qué sensación?
CARLOS	Casi no me atrevo a decírtelo... Es tan nueva para mí... Una sensación como de... desprecio.
JUANA	¡Carlos!
CARLOS	No lo pude evitar. ¡Ah! Y también me preguntó qué le ocurría a Elisita, y si había reñido con Miguelín. Por consideración a Miguelín no quise explicárselo a fondo.
JUANA	¡Pobre Elisa! Cuando estábamos en la mesa noté perfectamente que apenas comía. (*Breve pausa.*) Es raro que no esté por aquí.

(ELISA *no acusa estas palabras, aunque no está tan lejos como para no oírlas. Continúa abstraída en sus pensamientos. Tampoco ellos intuyen su presencia: el enlace parece haberse roto entre los ciegos.*)

CARLOS	Es ya tarde. Esto no tardará en llenarse, y seguramente se ha refugiado en algún rincón solitario. (*Súbitamente enardecido.*) ¡Y por ella, y por todos, y por ese imbécil de Miguelín también, hay que arreglar esto!
JUANA	¿De qué modo?

JANE	I don't know what to think... I consider myself partly to blame.
CHARLES	(*In a flat tone.*) You... to blame?
JANE	Yes. I've told you that on the first day of term I managed to talk him out of leaving. And now I think that maybe it would have been better if he had.
CHARLES	It would have; but we can still arrange things, eh?[23]
JANE	Perhaps.
CHARLES	Yesterday I had to tell Mr P. the same thing... it's surprising how much all this has affected him. He couldn't put his finger on anything specific, but he poured his worries out to me... He finds the boys more reserved and less determined than before. They're rather laid back in class competitions these days... I tried to cheer him up. Seeing him so indecisive made me feel sorry for him. Well, sorry... and something else very strange.
JANE	Very strange?... What?
CHARLES	I hardly dare tell you... it's new to me... but I had a feeling of, like ... contempt.
JANE	Charles!
CHARLES	I couldn't help it. Oh, and when he asked me as well what was wrong with Lisa, if she'd had a row with Mikey. For Mikey's sake, I didn't want to tell Mr P. the whole story.
JANE	Poor Lisa! When we were eating, I certainly noticed that she hardly touched a pick. (*A brief pause.*) It's strange that she isn't here. (LISA *does not register these words, although she is not too far away to hear them. She remains caught up in her thoughts. The other two do not sense her presence: the link between these blind people seems to have been broken.*)[24]
CHARLES	It's getting late. This place'll soon fill up, and she'll surely have hidden herself away in some quiet corner. (*Suddenly inflamed.*) For her sake, for everyone, and for that fool Mikey too, we've got to sort this out!
JANE	How?

CARLOS	Ignacio nos ha demostrado que la cordialidad y la dulzura son inútiles con él. Es agrio y despegado... ¡Está enfermo! Responde a la amistad con la maldad.
JUANA	Está intranquilo; carece de paz interior...
CARLOS	*No* tiene paz ni la quiere. (*Pausa grave.*) ¡Tendrá guerra!.
JUANA	(*Levantándose, súbitamente, para pasear su agitación.*) ¿Guerra?
CARLOS	¿Qué te pasa?
JUANA	(*Desde el primer término.*) Has pronunciado una palabra... tan odiosa... ¿No es mejor siempre la dulzura?
CARLOS	No conoces a Ignacio. En el fondo es cobarde; hay que combatirle. ¡Quién nos iba a decir cuando vino que, lejos de animarle, nos desuniría a nosotros! Porque perdemos posiciones, Juana. Posee una fuerza para el contagio con la que no contábamos.
JUANA	Yo pensé algún tiempo en buscarle una novia..., pero no la he encontrado. ¡Y qué gran solución sería!
CARLOS	Tampoco. Ignacio no es hombre a quien pueda cambiar ninguna mujer. Ahora está rodeado de compañeras, bien lo sabes... Van a él como atraídas por un imán. Y él las desdeña. Sólo nos queda un camino: desautorizarle ante los demás por la fuerza del razonamiento, hacerle indeseable a los compañeros. ¡Forzarle a salir de aquí!
JUANA	¡Qué fracaso para el centro!
CARLOS	¿Fracaso? La razón no puede fracasar, y nosotros la tenemos.
JUANA	(*Compungida.*) Sí... Pero una novia le regeneraría.
CARLOS	(*Cariñoso.*) Vamos, ven aquí... ¡Ven! (*Ella se acerca despacio. Él toma sus manos.*) Juanita mía, ¡me gustas tanto por tu bondad! Si fueras médico emplearías siempre bálsamos y nunca el escalpelo. (JUANA *se recuesta, sonriente, en el sillón y le besa.*) Nos hemos quedado solos para combatir, Juana. No desertes tú también.

(*Breve pausa.*)

JUANA	¿Por qué dices eso?
CARLOS	Por nada. Es que ahora te necesito más que nunca.

CHARLES	Iggy's shown us that being nice and sweet's a waste of time with him. He's bitter and unfriendly… He's sick. Give him friendship, and he gives you evil.
JANE	He's ill at ease; he lacks inner peace…
CHARLES	He neither has nor wants peace. (*A grave pause.*) He can have war, then![25]
JANE	(*Rising suddenly, to walk off her agitation.*) War?
CHARLES	What's the matter?
JANE	(*From Down-stage.*) You've uttered a really hateful word… Isn't gentleness always best?
CHARLES	You don't know Iggy. Deep down, he's a coward; we have to fight him. Who could have predicted when he came that, far from us cheering him up, he would divide us? We're losing ground, Jane. He's got a power of contagion we hadn't reckoned on![26]
JANE	At one stage I thought of getting him a girlfriend…, but I couldn't find one. That'd be a great solution!
CHARLES	No it wouldn't. Iggy's a guy no woman could change. Nowadays he's surrounded by females, as well you know… They go to him like he was a magnet. And he scorns them. There's only one way open to us: undermine him in front of all the others by the power of reason, make him an outcast. Force him to leave!
JANE	That'd be a real failure for the Centre!
CHARLES	A failure? Reason doesn't fail and we have it on our side.[27]
JANE	(*Pityingly.*) Yes… but a girlfriend'd make a new man of him.
CHARLES	(*Tenderly.*) Come over here… come on! (*She approaches slowly. He takes her hands.*) My Janey. I like you so because of your kindness! If you were a doctor, it'd be all balms and lotions, and no scalpel. (JANE, *smiling, lies back on the armchair and kisses him.*) We're on our own for this battle, Jane. Don't you desert too. (*A brief pause.*)
JANE	What makes you say that?
CHARLES	Nothing. It's just that now I need you more than ever.

(*Entran por el foro* IGNACIO *y los tres estudiantes.* IGNACIO *no ha abandonado su bastón, pero ha acentuado su desaliño: no lleva corbata.*)

ANDRÉS   Aquí, Ignacio.

(*Conduciéndolo a los sillones de la izquierda.*)

IGNACIO   ¿Vienen las chicas?
ALBERTO   No se las oye.
IGNACIO   Menos mal. Llegan a ponerse inaguantables.
ANDRÉS   No te preocupes por ellas. Anda, siéntate. (*Sacando una cajetilla.*) Toma un cigarrillo.
IGNACIO   No, gracias. (*Se sienta.*) ¿Para qué fumar? ¿Para imitar a los videntes?
ANDRÉS   Tienes razón. El primer pitillo se fuma por eso. Lo malo es que luego se coge el vicio. Tomad vosotros.

(*Da cigarrillos a los otros. Se sientan. Cada uno enciende con su cerilla y la tira en el cenicero.* CARLOS *crispa las manos sobre el sillón y* JUANA *se sienta en el sofá.*)

CARLOS   (*Con ligero tono de reto.*) Buenas tardes, amigos.
IGNACIO, ANDRÉS y ALBERTO   (*Con desgana.*) Hola.
PEDRO   Hola, Carlos. ¿Qué haces por aquí?
CARLOS   Aquí estoy, con Juana.

(IGNACIO *levanta la cabeza.*)

IGNACIO   Se está muy bien aquí. Tenemos un buen otoño.
ANDRÉS   Aún es pronto. El sol está dando en la terraza.
PEDRO   Bueno, Ignacio, prosigue con tu historia.
IGNACIO   ¿Dónde estábamos?
ALBERTO   Estábamos en que en aquel momento tropezaste.
IGNACIO   (*Se arrellana y suspira.*) Sí. Fue al bajar los escalones. Seguramente a vosotros os ha ocurrido alguna vez. Uno cuenta y cree que han terminado. Entonces se adelanta confiadamente el pie y se pega un gran pisotón en el suelo. Yo lo pegué y el corazón me dio un vuelco. Apenas podía tenerme en pie; las piernas se habían convertido en algodón, y las muchachas se estaban

(IGGY *and the three male students enter Up-stage.* IGGY *has not stopped using his stick, but has become even more untidy: he is not wearing a tie.*)

ANDY	This way, Iggy. (*Leading him to the armchairs on the Right.*)
IGGY	Are the girls coming?
AL	No sign of them.
IGGY	Just as well. They're becoming unbearable.
ANDY	Don't worry about them. Come on, sit down. (*Taking out a pack.*) Have a cigarette.
IGGY	No thanks. (*He sits down.*) What's the point of smoking? To imitate the seers?
ANDY	You're right. That's what happens with the first ciggie. The bad thing is, then you're hooked. Here. (*He gives cigarettes to the other two fellows. They sit down. Each of them lights up with a match which they throw in the ashtray.* CHARLES *clenches his hands on the armchair and* JANE *sits on the sofa.*)
CHARLES	(*In a slightly challenging tone.*) 'Afternoon, guys.
IGGY, ANDY & AL	(*Grudgingly.*) Hi.
PETE	Hi, Charles. What are you doing here?
CHARLES	Just hanging out with Jane. (IGGY *raises his head.*)
IGGY	It's nice here. We're having a fine Autumn.
ANDY	It's early days yet. The sun's hitting the terrace.
PETE	Ok, Iggy, get on with your story.
IGGY	Where was I?
AL	You got to the part where you fell.[28]
IGGY	(*Settles back and sighs.*) Ah, yes. It was going down the steps. Surely it has happened to you all at one time or another. You count and you think there are no more. Then you stick your foot out confidently and down you go on the ground with a thump. Well down I went and my stomach turned. I could hardly stand upright; my legs had turned to jelly, and the girls were laughing their

riendo a carcajadas. Era una risa limpia y sin malicia; pero a mí me traspasó. Y sentí que me ardía el rostro. Las muchachas trataban de cortar sus risas; no podían, y volvían a empezar. ¿Habéis notado que muchas veces las mujeres no pueden dejar de reír? Se ponen tan nerviosas, que les es imposible... Yo estaba a punto de llorar. ¡Sólo tenía quince años! Entonces me senté en un escalón y me puse a pensar. Intenté comprender por primera vez por qué estaba ciego y por qué tenía que haber ciegos. ¡Es abominable que la mayoría de las personas, sin valer más que nosotros, gocen, sin mérito alguno, de un poder misterioso que emana de sus ojos y con el que pueden abrazarnos y clavarnos el cuerpo sin que podamos evitarlo! Se nos ha negado ese poder de aprehensión de las cosas a distancia, y estamos por debajo, ¡sin motivo!, de los que viven ahí fuera. Aquella vieja cantinela de los ciegos que se situaban por las esquinas en tiempo de nuestros padres, cuando decían, para limosnear: «No hay prenda como la vista, hermanitos», no armoniza bien tal vez con nuestra tranquila vida de estudiantes; pero yo la creo mucho más sincera y más valiosa. Porque ellos no hacían como nosotros; no incurrían en la tontería de creerse normales.

(*A medida que* CARLOS *escuchaba a* IGNACIO, *su expresión de ira reprimida se ha acentuado.* JUANA *ha reflejado en su rostro una extraña identificación con las incidencias del relato.*)

ANDRÉS   (*Reservado.*) Acaso tengas razón... Yo he pensado también mucho en esas cosas. Y creo que con la ceguera no sólo carecemos de un poder a distancia, sino de un placer también. Un placer maravilloso, seguramente. ¿Cómo supones tú que será?

(MIGUELÍN, *que no ha perdido del todo su aire jovial, desemboca en la terraza por la izquierda. Pasa junto a* ELISA, *sin sentirla – ella se mueve con ligera aprensión –, y llega al interior a tiempo de escuchar las palabras de* IGNACIO.)

heads off. It was innocent laughter, no malice intended, but it really got to me. And I could feel my cheeks burning up. The girls tried to stop laughing; they couldn't, and they started up again. Have you noticed how women often can't stop laughing? They get so nervous that they can't... I was on the verge of tears. I was only fifteen years of age! Then I sat down on one of the steps and started thinking. I tried to understand for the first time in my life why I was blind and why there had to be blind people. It's terrible that most people, no better than us, enjoy, without having done anything at all to deserve it, the mysterious power flowing from their eyes, with which they can grasp and pierce our bodies without us being able to stop it! We've been denied that power of perception of things at a distance, and, for no reason at all, we're inferior to those who live out there! That old line that used to be said, in our fathers' day by blind men begging on the street corners, 'There's nothing like sight, brothers and sisters', doesn't quite gel perhaps with our cushy student lifestyle; but I think it's much more honest and valuable. Because those people back then didn't do what we do: they didn't indulge in the stupid notion of thinking that they were normal. (*While* CHARLES *has been listening to* IGGY, *his expression of repressed anger has grown more intense.* JANE*'s face has mirrored a strong sense of identification with the incidents in the story.*)

ANDY   (*Reticently.*) Maybe you're right... I've thought a lot too about those things. And I think that with blindness we're not only deprived of a power, but of a pleasure as well. A fantastic pleasure, no doubt. What do you think it'd be like? (MIKEY, *who has not totally lost his cheerful manner, appears on the terrace to the Right. He passes close by* LISA, *without sensing her presence – she moves slightly apprehensively – and makes it indoors in time to hear* IGGY*'s words.*)

IGNACIO   (*Accionando para él solo con sus manos llenas de anhelo y violencia, subraya inconscientemente la calidad táctil que sus presunciones ofrecen.*) Pienso que es como si por los ojos entrase continuamente un cosquilleo que fuese removiendo nuestros nervios y nuestras vísceras... y haciéndonos sentir más tranquilos y mejores.

ANDRÉS   (*Con un suspiro.*) Así debe de ser.

MIGUEL   ¡Hola, chicos!

(*Desde la terraza,* ELISA *levanta la cabeza, lleva las manos al pecho y se empieza a acercar.*)

PEDRO   Hola, Miguelín.

ANDRÉS   Llegas a tiempo para decirnos cómo crees tú que es el placer de ver.

MIGUEL   ¡Ah! Pues de un modo muy distinto a como lo ha explicado Ignacio. Pero nada de eso importa, porque a mí se me ha ocurrido hoy una idea genial – ¡no os riáis! –, y es la siguiente: nosotros no vemos. Bien. ¿Concebimos la vista? No. Luego la vista es inconcebible. Luego los videntes no ven tampoco.

(*Salvo* IGNACIO, *el grupo ríe a carcajadas.*)

PEDRO   ¿Pues qué hacen, si no ven?

MIGUEL   No os riáis, idiotas. ¿Qué hacen? Padecen una alucinación colectiva. ¡La locura de la visión! Los únicos seres normales en este mundo de locos somos nosotros.

(*Estallan otra vez las risas.* MIGUELÍN *ríe también.* ELISA *sufre.*)

IGNACIO   (*Cuya voz profunda y melancólica acalla las risas de los otros.*) Miguelín ha encontrado una solución, pero absurda. Nos permitiría vivir tranquilos si no supiéramos demasiado bien que la vista existe. *(Suspira.)* Por eso tu hallazgo no nos sirve.

MIGUEL   (*Con repentina melancolía en la voz.*) Pero, ¿verdad que es gracioso?

IGNACIO   (*Sonriente.*) Sí. Tú has sabido ocultar entre risas, como siempre, lo irreparable de tu desgracia.

IGGY	(*Gesturing to himself alone with hand movements full of yearning and violence, and unconsciously underlining the tactile quality of his intimations.*) I think it's like as if a tickling sensation was constantly coming in through our eyes, stirring our nerve ends and insides… and making us feel better and more relaxed.
ANDY	(*With a sigh.*) It must be like that.
MIKEY	Hi, guys! (*Out on the terrace,* LISA *raises her head and lifts her hands chest-high and begins to approach.*)
PETE	Hi, Mikey.
ANDY	You're just in time to tell us how you imagine the pleasure of seeing is.
MIKEY	Well now, I imagine it in a very different way from Iggy. But none of that matters, because I've had a brilliant idea today – don't laugh, now – this is it: We can't see. Ok. Can we conceive of sight? No. Then sight is inconceivable. Therefore the seers don't see either. (*Except for* IGGY, *the group bursts out laughing.*)[29]
PETE	Well, then, what do they do, if they don't see?
MIKEY	Don't laugh, you fools. What do they do? They suffer from a collective hallucination. The folly of sight! We're the only normal people in this world of madmen. (*Laughter breaks out again.* MIKEY *laughs too.* LISA *looks anguished.*)
IGGY	(*Whose deep, melancholic voice silences the others' laughter.*) Mikey has found a solution, but it's absurd. It would allow us to live at ease were it not for the fact that we know only too well that sight exists. (*He sighs.*) That's why your discovery's no good to us.
MIKEY	(*With a sudden melancholic tone in his voice.*) But, it's funny, isn't it?
IGGY	(*Smiling.*) Yes. Through laughter, as always, you've managed to conceal the awfulness of your affliction.

(*La seriedad de* MIGUELÍN *aumenta.*)

ELISA   (*Que no puede más.*) ¡Miguelín!
JUANA   ¡Elisa!
MIGUEL   (*Trivial.*) ¡Caramba, Juana! ¿Estabas aquí? ¿Y Carlos?
CARLOS   Aquí estoy también. Y si me lo permitís (*Apretando
             sobre el sillón la mano de* JUANA *en muda advertencia.*),
             me sentaré con vosotros.

(*Se sienta a la izquierda del grupo.*)

ELISA   ¡Miguelín, escucha! ¡Vamos a pasear al campo de
             deportes! ¡Se está muy bien ahora! ¿Quieres?
MIGUEL   (*Despegado.*) Elisita, si acabo de llegar de allí
             precisamente. Y ésta es una conversación muy
             interesante. ¿Por qué no te sientas con Juana?
JUANA   Ven conmigo, Elisa. Aquí tienes un sillón.

(ELISA *suspira y no dice nada. Se sienta junto a* JUANA, *quien la mima
y la conforta en su desaliento, hasta que el interés de la conversación
entre* IGNACIO *y* CARLOS *absorbe a las dos.*)

ALBERTO   ¿Nos escuchabas, Carlos?
CARLOS   Sí, Alberto. Todo era muy interesante.
ANDRÉS   ¿Y qué opinas tú de ello?
CARLOS   (*Con tono mesurado.*) No entiendo bien algunas
             cosas. Sabéis que soy un hombre práctico. ¿A qué fin
             razonable os llevaban vuestras palabras? Eso es lo que
             no comprendo. Sobre todo cuando no encuentro en ellas
             otra cosa que inquietud y tristeza.
MIGUEL   ¡Alto! También había risas... (*De nuevo con involuntaria
             melancolía.*) provocadas por la irreparable desgracia de
             este humilde servidor.

(*Risas.*)

CARLOS   (*Con tono de creciente decisión.*) Siento decirte,
             Miguelín, que a veces no eres nada divertido. Pero
             dejemos eso. (*Vibrante.*) A ti, Ignacio (*Éste se estremece
             ante el tono de* CARLOS.), a ti es a quien quiero preguntar
             algo: ¿quieres decir con lo que nos has dicho que los
             invidentes formamos un mundo aparte de los videntes?

	(MIKEY *becomes even more serious.*)
LISA	(*Who cannot contain herself.*) Mikey!
JANE	Lisa!
MIKEY	(*Making light of things.*) My God, Jane! You were here! And Charles?
CHARLES	I'm here too. And if you'll permit me (*Squeezing* JANE*'s hand against the sofa in a silent warning.*), I'll sit with you all. (*He sits down on the right of the group.*)
LISA	Listen, Mikey, let's go for a walk round the sports field! It's nice out there! 'You coming?
MIKEY	(*Distantly.*) Lisa, that's just where I've come from. And this is a very interesting conversation. Why don't you sit down with Jane?
JANE	Come over here with me, Lisa. Here's an armchair. (LISA *sighs and says nothing. She sits beside* JANE, *who fusses over her and comforts her in her defeated state, until interest in the conversation between* IGGY *and* CHARLES *captivates them both.*)
AL	Were you listening to us, Charles?
CHARLES	Yes, Al. It was all very interesting.
ANDY	And what do you think of it all?
CHARLES	(*In measured tones.*) There are some things I don't quite understand. You know I'm a practical kind of guy. To what sort of reasonable conclusion were your words leading you? That's what I don't understand. Especially when all I detect in them is worry and sadness.
MIKEY	Hold on! There was some laughter too… (*Again with involuntary melancholy.*) brought about by the awfulness of yours truly's affliction. (*Laughter.*)
CHARLES	(*In an increasingly determined tone.*) I'm sorry to say, Mikey, that sometimes you're not funny at all. But never mind that. (*Forcefully.*) It's you, Iggy (IGGY *shudders at* CHARLES*'s voice.*), it's you I want to ask a question: does all that you've said to us mean that you think that we non-seers form a separate world from the seers?

IGNACIO   (*Que parece asustado, carraspea.*) Pues... yo he querido decir...

CARLOS   (*Tajante.*) No, por favor. ¿Lo has querido decir, sí o no?

IGNACIO   Pues... sí. Un mundo aparte... y más desgraciado.

CARLOS   ¡Pues no es cierto! Nuestro mundo y el de ellos es el mismo. ¿Acaso no estudiamos como ellos? ¿Es que no somos socialmente útiles como ellos? ¿No tenemos también nuestras distracciones? ¿No hacemos deporte? (*Pausa breve.*) ¿No amamos, no nos casamos?

IGNACIO   (*Suave.*) ¿No vemos?

CARLOS   (*Violento.*) ¡No, no vemos! Pero ellos son mancos, cojos, paralíticos, están enfermos de los nervios, del corazón o del riñón; se mueren a los veinte años de tuberculosis o los asesinan en las guerras. O se mueren de hambre.

ALBERTO   Eso es cierto.

CARLOS   ¡Claro que es cierto! La desgracia está muy repartida entre los hombres, pero nosotros no formamos rancho aparte en el mundo. ¿Quieres una prueba definitiva? Los matrimonios entre nosotros y los videntes. Hoy son muchos; mañana serán la regla... Hace tiempo que habríamos conseguido mejores resultados si nos hubiésemos atrevido a pensar así en lugar de salmodiar lloronamente el «no hay prenda como la vista», de que hablabas antes. (*Severo, a los otros.*) Y me extraña mucho que vosotros, viejos ya en la institución, podáis dudarlo ni por un momento. (*Pausa breve.*) Se comprende que dude Ignacio... No sabe aún lo grande, lo libre y hermosa que es nuestra vida. No ha adquirido confianza; tiene miedo a dejar su bastón... ¡Sois vosotros quienes debéis ayudarle a confiar!

(*Pausa.*)

ANDRÉS   ¿Qué dices a eso, Ignacio?

IGNACIO   Las razones de Carlos son muy débiles. Pero esta conversación parece un pugilato. ¿No sería mejor dejarla? Yo te estimo, Carlos, y no quisiera...

IGGY	(*Seeming startled, clears his throat.*) Well... I meant that...
CHARLES	(*Emphatically.*) Come on, is that what you meant or not?
IGGY	Well... yes. A separate world... and a more unfortunate one.
CHARLES	Well, that's not right. Our world and theirs are the same. Don't we study like they do? Aren't we of use to society, as they are? Don't we have our amusements too? Don't we play sports? (*A brief pause.*) Don't we love and get married?
IGGY	(*Gently.*) Do we see?
CHARLES	(*Furiously.*) No, we don't see! But they get maimed, crippled, paralysed; they get sick with nerves, heart trouble or their kidneys; they die of TB at twenty or get killed in wars. They even die of starvation.
AL	That's true!
CHARLES	Of course it's true! Misfortunes are very well spread out among mankind, but we aren't a little clique separated from the rest of the world. Do you want definitive proof? Take marriages between ourselves and seers. There are lots of them nowadays; in the future they'll be the rule... In times gone by we'd have achieved more if we'd dared to think like that instead of cheerfully chanting the old line about 'There's nothing like sight' that you mentioned before. (*Sternly, to the others.*) And I'm surprised at you, the older hands here in the Centre, that you could doubt that even for a moment. (*A brief pause.*) You can understand Iggy's doubting... He doesn't yet know how great, free and fine life is here. He hasn't got confidence; he's afraid of doing without his stick... You're the people who ought to help him be confident! (*A pause.*)
ANDY	What do you say to that, Iggy?
IGGY	Charles's arguments are very weak. But this conversation seems like a punch-up. Wouldn't it be better to drop it? I really think a lot of you, Charles, and I wouldn't want to...

PEDRO	No, no. Debes contestarle.
IGNACIO	Es que...
CARLOS	(*Burlón, creyendo vencer.*) No te preocupes, hombre. Contéstame. No hay nada más molesto que un problema a medio resolver.
IGNACIO	Olvidas que, por desgracia, los grandes problemas no suelen resolverse.

(*Se levanta y sale del grupo.*)

ANDRÉS	¡No te marches!
CARLOS	(*Con aparente benevolencia.*) Déjale, Andrés... Es comprensible. No tiene todavía seguridad en sí mismo...
IGNACIO	(*Junto al velador de la derecha.*) Y por eso necesito mi bastón, ¿no?
CARLOS	Tú mismo lo dices...
IGNACIO	(*Cogiendo sin ruido el cenicero que hay sobre el velador y metiéndoselo en el bolsillo de la chaqueta.*) Todos lo necesitamos para no tropezar.
CARLOS	¡Lo que te hace tropezar es el miedo, el desánimo! Llevarás el bastón toda tu vida y tropezarás toda tu vida. ¡Atrévete a ser como nosotros! ¡Nosotros no tropezamos!
IGNACIO	Muy seguro estás de ti mismo. Tal vez algún día tropieces y te hagas mucho daño... Acaso más pronto de lo que crees. (*Pausa.*) Por lo demás, no pensaba marcharme. Deseo contestarte, pero permitidme todos que lo haga paseando... Así me parece que razono mejor. (*Ha tomado por su tallo el velador y marcha, marcando bien los golpes del bastón, al centro de la escena. Allí lo coloca suavemente, sin el menor ruido.*) Tú, Carlos, pareces querer decirnos que hay que atreverse a confiar; que la vida es la misma para nosotros y para los videntes.
CARLOS	Cabalmente.
IGNACIO	Confías demasiado. Tu seguridad es ilusoria... No resistiría el tropiezo más pequeño. Te ríes de mi bastón, pero mi bastón me permite pasear por aquí, como hago ahora, sin miedo a los obstáculos.

PETE	No, no. You must answer.
IGGY	It's just that…
CHARLES	(*Mockingly, thinking he's on top.*) Don't worry, mate. Answer. There's nothing more annoying than a half-solved problem.
IGGY	You're forgetting that, unfortunately, the really big problems can't usually be solved. (*He gets up and leaves the group.*)
ANDY	Don't go!
CHARLES	(*With ostensible largesse.*) Let him go, Andy… It's understandable. He's still not sure of himself…
IGGY	(*Near to the table on the Left.*) And that's why I need my stick, right?
CHARLES	You've said it yourself…
IGGY	(*Silently lifting the ashtray off the small table and putting it in his jacket pocket.*) We all need one so we don't stumble about.
CHARLES	What makes you stumble is fear, and dejection! You'll carry the stick all your days and stumble around the place all your days. Dare to be like us! We don't stumble!
IGGY	You're very sure of yourself. Maybe some day you'll fall and do yourself a serious injury… Sooner than you think perhaps. (*A pause.*) Anyway, I wasn't thinking of going. I want to answer you, but allow me to do so while I walk around… I think I can reason better like that. (*He has lifted the table by its leg and walks, while tapping firmly with his stick, to Centre-stage, where he gently sets the table down without the slightest sound.*)[30] So, Charles, you seem to want to tell us that we must dare to be confident, that life is the same for us as it is for the seers…
CHARLES	Exactly.
IGGY	You're too cocky. Your security is an illusion… it wouldn't stand up to the slightest little stumble. You laugh at my stick, but my stick lets me walk about here, as I'm doing now, without fearing obstacles.

(Se dirige al primer término derecho y se vuelve. El velador se encuentra exactamente en la línea que le une con CARLOS.*)*

CARLOS	*(Riendo.)* ¿Qué obstáculos? ¡Aquí no hay ninguno! ¿Te das cuenta de tu cobardía? Si usases sin temor de tu conocimiento del sitio, como hacemos nosotros, tirarías ese palo.
IGNACIO	No quiero tropezar.
CARLOS	*(Exaltado.)* ¡Si no puedes tropezar! Aquí todo está previsto. No hay un solo rincón de la casa que no conozcamos. El bastón está bien para la calle, pero aquí...
IGNACIO	Aquí también es necesario. ¿Cómo podemos saber nosotros, pobres ciegos, lo que nos acecha alrededor?
CARLOS	¡No somos pobres! ¡Y lo sabemos perfectamente! *(*IGNACIO *ríe sin rebozo.)* ¡No te rías!
IGNACIO	Perdona, pero... me resulta tan pueril tu optimismo... Por ejemplo, si yo te pidiera que te levantases y vinieses muy aprisa a donde me encuentro, quieres hacernos creer que lo harías sin miedo...
CARLOS	*(Levantándose de golpe.)* ¡Naturalmente! ¿Quieres que lo haga?

(Pausa.)

IGNACIO	*(Grave.)* Sí, por favor. Muy de prisa, no lo olvides.
CARLOS	¡Ahora mismo!

(Todos los ciegos adelantan la cabeza, en escucha. CARLOS *da unos pasos rápidos, pero de pronto la desconfianza crispa su cara y disminuye la marcha, extendiendo los brazos. No tarda en palpar el velador, y una expresión de odio brutal le invade.)*

IGNACIO	Vienes muy despacio.
CARLOS	*(Que, bordeando el velador, ha avanzado con los puños cerrados hasta enfrentarse con* IGNACIO.*)* No lo creas. Ya estoy aquí.
IGNACIO	Has vacilado.
CARLOS	¡Nada de eso! Vine seguro de convencerte de lo vano

(*He heads Down-Left and turns. The table is directly in line between himself and* CHARLES.)

CHARLES	(*Laughing.*) What obstacles? There are none here! Do you realise how cowardly you are? If you were fearless and used your knowledge of the place as we do, you'd throw that stick away.
IGGY	I don't want to fall.
CHARLES	(*Impassioned.*) You can't fall! Everything's been foreseen here. There isn't a single corner of the place that we don't know. The stick's fine in the street, but here...
IGGY	We need it here as well. How can we poor blind people know what might be lying in wait for us?
CHARLES	We're not poor! And we know full well! (IGGY *laughs openly.*) Don't laugh!
IGGY	Sorry, but... your optimism seems so childish to me... For instance, if I asked you to get up and come over to me very quickly, do you mean to tell us that you'd do it with no fear...
CHARLES	(*Jumping to his feet.*) Sure thing! Do you want me to? (*Pause.*)
IGGY	(*Solemnly.*) Yes, please. Very quickly, don't forget.
CHARLES	Here I come! (*All the others crane forward to listen.* CHARLES *takes a few quick steps, but suddenly his face hardens with misgivings and he slows down, putting out his arms. He soon feels the table and a brutal hatred contorts his face.*)
IGGY	You're moving very slowly.
CHARLES	(*Rounding the table, he moves with his fists clenched to confront* IGGY.) Not at all. Here I am.
IGGY	You hesitated there.
CHARLES	No way. I did it confident of showing you that there's

de tus miedos. Y... te habrás persuadido... de que no hay obstáculos por en medio.

IGNACIO   (*Triunfante.*) Pero te dio miedo. ¡No lo niegues! (*A los demás.*) Le dio miedo. ¿No le oísteis vacilar y pararse?

MIGUEL   Hay que reconocerlo, Carlos. Todos lo advertimos.

CARLOS   (*Rojo.*) ¡Pero no lo hice por miedo! Lo hice porque de pronto comprendí...

IGNACIO   ¡Qué! ¿Acaso que podía haber obstáculos? Pues si no llamas a eso miedo, llámalo como quieras.

MIGUEL   ¡Un tanto para Ignacio!

CARLOS   (*Dominándose.*) Es cierto. No fue miedo, pero hubo una causa que..., que no puedo explicar. Esta prueba es nula.

IGNACIO   (*Benévolo.*) No tengo inconveniente en concedértelo. (*Mientras habla se encamina al grupo para sentarse de nuevo.*) Pero aún he de contestar a tus argumentos... Estudiamos, sí (*A todos.*); la décima parte de las cosas que estudian los videntes. Hacemos deportes..., menos nueve décimas partes de ellos. (*Se ha sentado plácidamente.* CARLOS, *que permanece inmóvil en el primer término, cruza los brazos tensos para contenerse.*) Y en cuanto al amor...

ALBERTO   Eso no podrás negarlo.

IGNACIO   El amor es algo maravilloso. El amor, por ejemplo, entre Carlos y Juana. (JUANA, *que ha seguido angustiada las peripecias de la disputa, se sobresalta.*) ¡Pero esa maravilla no pasa de ser una triste parodia del amor entre los videntes! Porque ellos poseen al ser amado por entero. Son capaces de englobarle en una mirada. Nosotros poseemos... a pedazos. Una caricia, el arrullo momentáneo de la voz... En realidad no nos amamos. Nos compadecemos y tratamos de disfrazar esa triste piedad con alegres tonterías, llamándola amor. Creo que sabría mejor si no la disfrazásemos.

MIGUEL   ¡Segundo tanto para Ignacio!

CARLOS   (*Conteniéndose.*) Me parece que has olvidado contestar a algo muy importante...

nothing to your fears. And... now you'll maybe realise... that there are no obstacles in the way.

IGGY (*Triumphantly.*) But you were afraid. Don't deny it! (*To the others.*) He was afraid. Didn't you hear him hesitate and stop?

MIKEY You've got to admit it, Charles. We were all aware of it.

CHARLES (*Reddening.*) But it wasn't because I was afraid. It was because I suddenly realised...

IGGY What? That there might just be obstacles? Well, if you don't call that being afraid, call it what you want.

MIKEY One-nil to Iggy!

CHARLES (*Controlling himself.*) Ok, it wasn't fear, but there was a reason that... I can't explain. This experiment is null and void.

IGGY (*Generously.*) Fair enough, I accept that. (*As he speaks he walks towards the group to sit down again.*) But I've still to answer the points you raised... We study, that's true (*To everyone.*): about 10% of the things seers study. We do sports..., bar 90% of them. (*He has sat down calmly.* CHARLES, *who hasn't moved from Down-stage, folds his arms tightly to control himself.*) As for love...

AL You can't deny that.

IGGY Love is something marvellous. The love between Charles and Jane, for instance. (JANE, *who has been following the ups and downs of the debate, is startled.*) But that marvel is no more than a sad parody of love between seers. Because they possess the one they love completely. They can take that person in with a single glance. We possess... bits of the person. A caress, a fleeting murmur of the voice... The truth is, we don't love each other at all. We feel sorry for each other and try to disguise that pity with cheerful frivolities, calling it love. I think it'd be better all round if we didn't disguise it.

MIKEY Two-nil to Iggy.

CHARLES (*Restraining himself.*) I think you've forgotten to answer one very important point...

IGNACIO	Puede ser.
CARLOS	Los matrimonios entre videntes e invidentes, ¿no prueban que nuestro mundo y el de ellos es el mismo? ¿No son una prueba de que el amor que sentimos y hacemos sentir no es una parodia?
IGNACIO	¡Ja, ja, ja! Yo no quisiera que mis palabras se interpretasen mal por alguien...
ANDRÉS	Todos te prometemos discreción.

(DOÑA PEPITA *avanza por la derecha de la terraza hacia la portalada, mirándolos tras los cristales. Al oír su nombre se detiene.*)

IGNACIO	La región del optimismo donde Carlos sueña no le deja apreciar la realidad. (*A* CARLOS.) Por eso no te has enterado de un detalle muy significativo que todos sabemos por las visitas. Muy significativo. Doña Pepita y don Pablo se casaron porque don Pablo necesitaba un bastón (*Golpea el suelo con el suyo.*); pero, sobre todo (*Se detiene.*), por una de esas cosas que los ciegos no comprendemos, pero que son tan importantes para los videntes. Porque... ¡doña Pepita es muy fea!

(*Un silencio. Poco a poco, la idea les complace. Ríen hasta estallar en grandes carcajadas.* CARLOS, *violento, no sabe qué decir.*)

MIGUEL	¡Tercer tanto para Ignacio!

(*Arrecian las carcajadas.* CARLOS *se retuerce las manos.* JUANA *ha apoyado la cabeza en las manos y está ensimismada.* DOÑA PEPITA, *que inclinó la cabeza con tristeza, se sobrepone e interviene.*)

DOÑA PEPITA	(*Cordial.*) ¡Buenas tardes, hijitos! Les encuentro muy alegres. (*A su voz, las risas cesan de repente.*) Algún chiste de Miguelín, probablemente... ¿No es eso?

(*Todos se levantan, conteniendo algunos la risa de nuevo.*)

MIGUEL	Lo acertó usted, doña Pepita.
DOÑA PEPITA	Pues le voy a reñir por hacerles perder el tiempo de ese

IGGY	Maybe.
CHARLES	Don't marriages between seers and non-seers prove that our world and theirs are one and the same? Don't they prove that the love we feel and inspire isn't a parody?
IGGY	Sheer pity! As in the other cases.
CHARLES	So, you would dare to suggest that Mr and Mrs P. never loved each other?
IGGY	A-ha! I wouldn't like my words to be misinterpreted by anyone…
ANDY	We all promise to be discreet. (MRS P. *moves on the Left of the terrace towards the door, watching them through the glass. On hearing her name, she stops.*)
IGGY	The optimism zone where Charles dreams his life away doesn't allow him to get a handle on reality. (*To* CHARLES.) So that's why you haven't latched onto one very significant detail that we've picked up from the visits we get. It's very significant. Mr and Mrs P. got married because Mr P. needed a stick (*He taps the floor loudly with his own.*); but, above all, because (*He stops.*) because of one of those things that we blind people don't understand, but which are so important to seers. Because… Mrs P. is brute ugly! (*Silence. The idea tickles their fancy. They laugh until their laughter becomes uproarious.* CHARLES, *very angry, does not know what to say.*)[31]
MIKEY	Three-nil to Iggy! (*Their hoots of laughter increase.* CHARLES *wrings his hands.* JANE *has put her head in her hands and is in a world of her own.* MRS P., *who had bowed her head sadly, pulls herself together and intervenes.*)
MRS P.	(*Cordially.*) Good afternoon, everyone! You seem very cheerful. (*At the sound of her voice the laughter suddenly stops.*) One of Mikey's jokes, no doubt… was that what it was? (*They all stand up, some of them trying not to laugh again.*)
MIKEY	You got it, Mrs P.
MRS P.	Then I'll have to tell him off for making you waste time

modo. Van a dar las tres y aún no han ido a ensayar al campo... ¿A qué altura van a dejar el nombre del centro en el concurso de patín? ¡Vamos! ¡Al campo todo el mundo!

MIGUEL   Usted perdone.

DOÑA PEPITA   Perdonado. Pórtese bien ahora en la pista. Y ustedes, señoritas, vengan conmigo a la terraza a tomar el aire. (*Los estudiantes van desfilando hacia la terraza y desaparecen por la izquierda, entre risas reprimidas.* CARLOS, IGNACIO, JUANA *y* ELISA *permanecen.* DOÑA PEPITA *se dirige entonces a* CARLOS *con especial ternura. El estudiante es para ella el alumno predilecto de la casa. Tal vez el hijo de carne que no llegó a tener con* DON PABLO... *Acaso esté un poco enamorada de él sin saberlo.*) Carlos, don Pablo quiere hablarle.

CARLOS   Ahora voy, doña Pepita. En cuanto termine un asuntillo con Ignacio.

DOÑA PEPITA   Y usted, ¿no quiere patinar, Ignacio? ¿Cuándo se decide a dejar el bastón?

IGNACIO   No me atrevo, doña Pepita. Además, ¿para qué?

DOÑA PEPITA   Pues, hijo, ¿no ve a sus compañeros cómo van y vienen sin él?

IGNACIO   No, señora. Yo no veo nada.

DOÑA PEPITA   (*Seca.*) Claro que no. Perdone. Es una forma de hablar... ¿Vamos, señoritas?

JUANA   Cuando guste.

DOÑA PEPITA   (*Enlazando por el talle a las dos muchachas.*) Ahí se quedan ustedes. (*Afectuosa.*) No olvide a don Pablo, Carlos.

CARLOS   Descuide. Voy en seguida.

(DOÑA PEPITA *y las muchachas avanzan hacia la barandilla, donde se recuestan.* DOÑA PEPITA *acciona vivamente, explicando a las ciegas las incidencias del patinaje.* IGNACIO *vuelve a sentarse. Una pausa.*)

IGNACIO   Tú dirás.

(CARLOS *no dice nada. Se acerca al velador y lo coge para devolverlo, con ostensible ruido, a su primitivo lugar. Después se enfrenta con* IGNACIO.)

	like this. It's almost three o'clock and you haven't been out training on the field yet... What's going to happen to the Centre's good name in the skating competition? Let's go! Out to the field, all of you!
MIKEY	Sorry!
MRS P.	That's ok. Behave yourself now on the skating rink. And you ladies come out onto the terrace with me to get some air. (*The students file out towards the terrace and disappear off Right, amid suppressed laughter.* CHARLES, IGGY, JANE *and* LISA *remain.* MRS P. *addresses* CHARLES *with special affection. He is her favourite student, perhaps the child herself and* MR P. *never managed to have... unwittingly she is maybe a little in love with him.*)[32] Charles, Mr P. wants to speak to you.
CHARLES	Right away, Mrs P. As soon as I've finished a little business with Iggy.
MRS P.	And what about you, Iggy, don't you want to skate? When are you going to get round to doing without that stick?
IGGY	I daren't, Mrs P. Anyway, what's the point?
MRS P.	But can't you see how all your friends come and go without one?
IGGY	No, Mrs P. I can't see anything.
MRS P.	(*Drily.*) Of course not. Sorry. It's just a figure of speech... Shall we go, ladies?
JANE	When you're ready.
MRS P.	(*Taking the two girls by the waist.*) We'll leave you two here then. (*Affectionately.*) Don't forget Mr P., Charles.
CHARLES	No problem. I'll go in just a moment. (MRS P. *and the girls go as far as the terrace railing, and lean on it.* MRS P. *gestures vividly, explaining to her blind charges what is happening on the skating rink.* IGGY *sits down again. A pause.*)
IGGY	Well then, go on. (CHARLES *says nothing. He goes over to the small table and picks it up to return it to its original place, deliberately making a noise. Then he confronts* IGGY.)

CARLOS   (*Seco.*) ¿Dónde has dejado el cenicero?
IGNACIO   (*Sonriendo.*) ¡Ah!, sí. Se me olvidaba. Tómalo.

(*Se lo alarga.* CARLOS *palpa en el vacío y lo atrapa bruscamente.*)

CARLOS   ¡No sé si te das cuenta de que estoy a punto de
              agredirte!
IGNACIO   No tendrías más razón aunque lo hicieras.

(CARLOS *se contiene. Después va a dejar el cenicero en su sitio, con un
sonoro golpe, y vuelve al lado de* IGNACIO.)

CARLOS   (*Resollando.*) Escucha, Ignacio. Hablemos lealmente. Y
              con la mayor voluntad de entendernos.
IGNACIO   Creo entenderte muy bien.
CARLOS   Me refiero a entendernos en la práctica.
IGNACIO   No es muy fácil.
CARLOS   De acuerdo. Pero ¿no lo crees necesario?
IGNACIO   ¿Por qué?
CARLOS   (*Con impaciencia reprimida.*) Procuraré explicarme.
              Ya que no pareces inclinado a abandonar tu pesimismo,
              para mí merece todos los respetos. ¡Pero encuentro
              improcedente que intentes contagiar a los demás! ¿Qué
              derecho tienes a eso?
IGNACIO   No intento nada. Me limito a ser sincero, y ese contagio de
              que me hablas no es más que el despertar de la sinceridad
              de cada cual. Me parece muy conveniente, porque aquí
              había muy poca. ¿Quieres decirme, en cambio, qué
              derecho te asiste para recomendar constantemente la
              alegría, el optimismo y todas esas zarandajas?
CARLOS   Ignacio, sabes que son cosas muy distintas. Mis palabras
              pueden servir para que nuestros compañeros consigan
              una vida relativamente feliz. Las tuyas no lograrán
              más que destruir; llevarlos a la desesperación, hacerles
              abandonar sus estudios.

(DOÑA PEPITA *interpela desde la terraza a los que patinan en el campo.*
IGNACIO *y* CARLOS *se interrumpen y escuchan.*)

CHARLES	(*Curtly.*) Where have you put the ashtray?
IGGY	(*Smiling.*) Oh, yeah! I forgot. Here you are. (*He holds it out.* CHARLES *feels for it and snatches it off him.*)
CHARLES	I don't know if you realise that I've a mind to land one on you!
IGGY	Doing that wouldn't make you any more right. (CHARLES *controls himself. Then he returns the ashtray to its place with a loud clank and comes back beside* IGGY.)[33]
CHARLES	(*Breathing heavily.*) Listen, Iggy. Let's have a straight talk and try to understand each other.
IGGY	I think I understand you very well.
CHARLES	I mean a practical understanding.
IGGY	That won't be very easy.
CHARLES	Agreed. But, don't you think it's necessary?
IGGY	Why?
CHARLES	(*Repressing his impatience.*) I'll try to explain myself. I can respect the fact that you don't seem inclined to give up your pessimistic outlook. But I think it's wrong that you should try to infect the others. What right do you have to do that?
IGGY	I'm not trying anything of the sort. I'm only being sincere and this infecting you're talking about is nothing more than sincerity's wake-up call for everyone. It seems like a very good thing to me, because there was very little of it here. So, will you tell me, then, what right you have to be always prescribing happiness, optimism and all that nonsense?
CHARLES	Iggy, you know that's a totally different ball game. My words may help to give our fellow students a relatively happy life. Yours can only destroy, make them despair and give up their studies. (MRS P. *calls out from the terrace to those who are skating below,* IGGY *and* CHARLES *break off to listen.*)

DOÑA PEPITA   ¡Se ha caído usted ya dos veces, Miguelín! Eso está muy mal. ¿Y a usted, Andrés, qué le pasa? ¿Por qué no se lanza?... Vaya. Otro que se cae. Están ustedes cada día más inseguros...

CARLOS   ¿Lo oyes?

IGNACIO   ¿Y qué?

CARLOS   ¡Qué tú eres el culpable!

IGNACIO   ¿Yo?

CARLOS   ¡Tú, Ignacio! Y yo te invito, amistosamente, a reflexionar... y a colaborar para mantener limpio el centro de problemas y de ruina. Creo que a todos nos interesa.

IGNACIO   ¡A mí no me interesa! Este centro está fundado sobre una mentira.

(DOÑA PEPITA, *con las manos en los hombros de las ciegas, las besa cariñosamente y se va por la derecha de la terraza.* JUANA *y* ELISA *se emparejan.*)

CARLOS   ¿Qué mentira?

IGNACIO   La de que somos seres normales.

CARLOS   ¡Ahora no discutiremos eso!

IGNACIO   (*Levantándose.*) ¡No discutiremos nada! No hay acuerdo posible entre tú y yo. Hablaré lo que quiera y no renunciaré a ninguna conquista que se me ponga en mi camino. ¡A ninguna!

CARLOS   (*Engarfia las manos. Se contiene.*) Está bien. Adiós.

(*Se va rápidamente por la derecha.* IGNACIO *queda solo. Silba melancólicamente unas notas del adagio del «Claro de luna». A poco, apoya las manos en el bastón y reclina la cabeza. Breve pausa.* LOLITA *entra por la terraza. A poco, entra por la derecha* ESPERANZA, *y la faz de cada una se ilumina al sentir los pasos de la otra. Avanzan hasta encontrarse y, casi a un tiempo, exclaman:*)

LOLITA   ¡Ignacio!

ESPERANZA   ¡Ignacio!

(*Éste se inmoviliza y no responde. Ellas ríen con alguna vergüenza, defraudadas.*)

MRS P.	You've fallen twice now, Mikey. That's a very poor show. And what's up with you, Andy? Why don't you give it a go?… My goodness! There's another one down. You're getting shakier every day…
CHARLES	Hear that?
IGGY	So?
CHARLES	You're to blame!
IGGY	Me?
CHARLES	Yes you, Iggy! And I'd ask you, as a friend, to think on… and help to keep the centre free from problems and destruction. I think that's in everyone's interest.
IGGY	Not mine. This Centre's founded on a lie.[34] (MRS P., *with her hands on the girls' shoulders, kisses them affectionately and goes out by the terrace to the Left.* JANE *and* LISA *link arms.*)
CHARLES	What lie?
IGGY	The one that says we're normal human beings.
CHARLES	Let's not go into that now!
IGGY	(*Getting up.*) We don't go into anything! Agreement between you and me is impossible. I'll say what I want and I'll let nothing get in my way. Nothing!
CHARLES	(*He clenches his fist and controls himself.*) Fine. Goodbye. (*He exits quickly to the Left.* IGGY *is alone. He melancholically whistles a few bars of the adagio from the 'Moonlight Sonata'. Thereafter he rests his hands on his stick and bows his head. A short pause.* LINDA *enters by the terrace. Then* HOPE *enters from the Left and their faces light up when each senses the steps of the other. They approach until they meet and, almost simultaneously, they exclaim:*)
LINDA	Iggy!
HOPE	Iggy! (IGGY *freezes and does not reply. The girls laugh rather shamefacedly, and are disappointed.*)

LOLITA	Tampoco está aquí.
ESPERANZA	(*Triste.*) Nos evita.
LOLITA	¿Tú crees?
ESPERANZA	Habla con nosotras por condescendencia..., pero nos desprecia. Sabe que no le entendemos.
LOLITA	¿No será que haya... alguna mujer?
ESPERANZA	Lo habríamos notado.
LOLITA	¡Quién sabe! Es tan hermético... Tal vez haya una mujer.
ESPERANZA	Vamos a buscar en el salón.
LOLITA	Vamos.

(*Salen por la izquierda, llamándolo. Pausa.* JUANA *y* ELISA *discutían algo en la terraza.* ELISA *está muy alterada; intenta desprenderse de* JUANA *para entrar en el fumadero y ésta trata de retenerla.*)

ELISA	(*Todavía en la terraza.*) ¡Déjame! Estoy ya harta de Ignacio.

(*Se separa y cruza la portalada, mientras* IGNACIO *levanta la cabeza.*)

JUANA	(*Tras ella.*) Vamos, tranquilízate. Siéntate aquí.
ELISA	¡No quiero!
JUANA	Siéntate...

(*La sienta cariñosamente en el sofá y se acomoda a su lado.*)

ELISA	¡Le odio! ¡Le odio!
JUANA	Un momento, Elisita. (*Alzando la voz.*) ¿Hay alguien aquí?

(IGNACIO *no contesta.* JUANA *coge una mano de su amiga.*)

ELISA	¡Cómo le odio!
JUANA	No es bueno odiar...
ELISA	Me ha quitado a Miguelín y nos quitará la paz a todos. ¡Mi Miguelín!
JUANA	Volverá. No lo dudes. Él te quiere. ¡Si, en realidad, no ha pasado nada! Un poco indiferente tal vez, estos días..., porque Miguelín fue siempre una veleta para las novedades. Ignacio es para él una distracción pasajera.

LINDA	He's not here either.
HOPE	(*Sadly*.) He's avoiding us.
LINDA	You think so?
HOPE	He just about talks to us and no more…, but he despises us. He knows we don't understand him.
LINDA	It wouldn't be because there's… some other girl?
HOPE	We'd have noticed.
LINDA	Who knows? He's so secretive… maybe there is a girl.
HOPE	Let's go and look in the lounge.
LINDA	Yes, let's. (*They exit right, calling him. A pause.* JANE *and* LISA *have been arguing about something out on the terrace.* LISA *is very upset; she tries to break away from* JANE *to go back into the common room and* JANE *tries to hold her back.*)
LISA	(*Still on the terrace.*) Leave me alone! I'm fed up with Iggy. (*She gets away and comes through the doorway, as* IGGY *lifts his head.*)
JANE	(*Following her.*) Right now, calm down. Sit down here.
LISA	I don't want to!
JANE	Sit down… (*Affectionately, she makes* LISA *sit on the sofa and settles in beside her.*)
LISA	I hate him! I hate him!
JANE	Just a minute, Lisa. (*Raising her voice.*) Is there anyone there? (IGGY *does not answer.* JANE *takes her friend's hand.*)
LISA	God, how I hate him!
JANE	It's not good to hate…
LISA	He's taken Mikey from me and he'll take away the peace of mind of all of us. My Mikey!
JANE	He'll be back. Don't doubt it. He loves you. I'm telling you, nothing's really happened! He's a little distant perhaps, these days… but Mikey was always a bit giddy about anything new. Iggy's a passing phase for him.

¡Y, en fin de cuentas, es un hombre! Si tuvieras que sufrir alguna veleidad de Miguelín con otra chica... Y aun eso no significaría que hubiera dejado de quererte.

ELISA   ¡Preferiría que me engañase con otra chica!

JUANA   ¡Qué dices, mujer!

ELISA   Sí. Esto es peor. Ese hombre le ha sorbido el seso y yo no tengo ya lugar en sus pensamientos.

JUANA   Creo que exageras.

ELISA   No... Pero oye, ¿no hay nadie aquí?

JUANA   No.

ELISA   Me parecía... (*Pausa. Volviendo a su tono de exaltación.*) Te lo dije el primer día, Juanita. Ese hombre está cargado de maldad. ¡Cómo lo adiviné! ¡Y esa afectación de Cristo martirizado que emplea para ganar adeptos! Los hombres son imbéciles. Y Miguelín, el más tonto de todos. ¡Pero yo le quiero!

(*Llora en silencio.*)

JUANA   Te oigo Elisa. No llores...

ELISA   (*Levantándose para pasear su angustia.*) ¡Es que le quiero, Juana!

JUANA   Lo que Miguelín necesita es un poco de indiferencia por tu parte. No le persigas tanto.

ELISA   Ya sé que me pongo en ridículo. No lo puedo remediar.

(*Se para junto a* IGNACIO, *que no respira, y seca sus ojos por última vez para guardar el pañuelo.*)

JUANA   ¡Inténtalo! Así volverá.

ELISA   ¿Cómo voy a intentarlo con ese hombre entre nosotros? Su presencia me anula... ¡ Ah! ¡Con qué gusto le abofetearía! ¡Quisiera saber qué se propone!

(*Engarfia las manos en el aire. Mas de pronto comienza a volverse lentamente hacia* IGNACIO, *sin darse cuenta todavía de que siente su presencia.*)

JUANA   No se propone nada. Sufre... y nosotros no sabemos curar su sufrimiento. En el fondo es digno de compasión.

	And, at the end of the day, he's a man! If you had to put up with Mikey flying his kite with another girl... And even that wouldn't mean that he'd stopped loving you.
LISA	I'd rather he cheated on me with another girl!
JANE	Come on now!
LISA	I mean it. This is worse. Iggy has bowled him over and he never even thinks about me anymore.
JANE	I think you're overstating it.
LISA	No, I'm not... but listen, is there someone there?
JANE	No.
LISA	I thought... (*A pause. Reverting to her excited tone.*) I told you that first day, Jane. That guy is really evil. I sensed it! And that Christ crucified show he puts on to get disciples![35] Men are fools. And Mikey's the daftest of the lot. But I love him! (*She weeps silently.*)
JANE	I hear what you're saying, Lisa. Don't cry...
LISA	(*Getting up in an attempt to walk off her anxiety.*) I really love him, Jane!
JANE	What Mikey needs is a little indifference from you. Don't chase after him so much.
LISA	I know I'm making a fool of myself. I can't help it. (*She stops beside* IGGY, *who holds his breath, and she dries her eyes for the last time, putting her handkerchief away.*)
JANE	Try. Then he'll come back.
LISA	How am I going to try with that guy between us? His very presence blots me out... ooh, I'd love to hit him! I'd like to know what he's up to! (*She raises her fists in the air. But suddenly she starts to turn slowly towards* IGGY, *without yet realising that she senses his presence.*)
JANE	He's not up to anything. He's suffering... and we don't know how to cure his suffering. Deep down, he's worthy of our compassion.

(*Las palabras de* JUANA *hacen volver otra vez la cabeza a* ELISA. *No ha llegado a sospechar nada.*)

ELISA	(*Avanzando hacia* JUANA.) Le compadeces demasiado. Es un egoísta. ¡Que sufra solo y no haga sufrir a los demás!
JUANA	(*Sonriente.*) Anda, siéntate y no te alteres. (*Se levanta y va hacia ella.*) Acusas a Ignacio de egoísta. ¿Y qué va a hacer, si sufre? También convendría menos egoísmo por nuestra parte. Hay que ser caritativos con las flaquezas ajenas y aliviarlas con nuestra dulzura...

(*Breve pausa.*)

ELISA	(*De pronto, exaltada, oprimiendo los brazos de* JUANA.) ¡No, no, Juana! ¡Eso no!
JUANA	(*Alarmada.*) ¿Qué?
ELISA	¡Eso, no, querida mía! ¡Eso no!
JUANA	¡Pero habla! No, ¿el qué?
ELISA	¡Tu simpatía por Ignacio!
JUANA	(*Molesta.*) ¿Qué dices?
ELISA	¡Prométeme ser fuerte! ¡Por amor a Carlos, prométemelo! (*Zarandeándola.*) ¡Prométemelo, Juana!
JUANA	(*Fría.*) No digas tonterías. Yo quiero a Carlos y no pasará nada. No sé qué piensas que pueda ocurrir.
ELISA	¡Todo! ¡Todo puede ocurrir! ¡Ese hombre me ha quitado a Miguelín y tú estás en peligro! ¡Prométeme evitarlo! ¡ Por Carlos, prométemelo!
JUANA	(*Muy alterada.*) ¡Elisa, cállate inmediatamente! ¡No te consiento...!

(*Se separa de ella con brusquedad. Pausa.*)

ELISA	(*Lenta, separándose.*) ¡Ah! ¡Soy tu mejor amiga y no me consientes! ¡También ha hecho presa en ti! ¡Estás en manos de ese hombre y no te das cuenta!
JUANA	¡Elisa!
ELISA	¡Me das lástima! ¡Y me da lástima Carlos, porque va a sufrir como yo sufro!

(JANE*'s words make* LISA *turn her head again. She still does not suspect anything.*)

LISA   (*Moving towards* JANE.) You're too soft on him. He's a selfish guy. Let him suffer alone and not make others suffer.

JANE   (*Smiling.*) Come on, sit down and don't get upset. (*She gets up and goes towards* LISA.) You say Iggy's selfish. But what can he do, if he's suffering? It'd be better too if we were less selfish ourselves. We have to be charitable with other people's weaknesses and try to offset them with our kindness… (*A brief pause.*)

LISA   (*Suddenly, in an excited state, holding* JANE*'s arms down.*) No, no, Jane! No way!

JANE   (*Alarmed.*) What?

LISA   Not that, darling! No, not that!

JANE   What do you mean, not that?

LISA   Your feelings for Iggy!

JANE   (*Annoyed.*) What are you saying?

LISA   Promise me you'll be strong! Out of love for Charles, promise me! (*Shaking her.*) Promise me, Jane.

JANE   (*Coldly.*) Don't talk nonsense. I love Charles, end of story. I don't know what you're thinking could happen.

LISA   Anything! Anything could happen! That guy's taken my Mikey and you're in danger! Promise me you won't let it happen! For Charles's sake, promise me!

JANE   (*Very annoyed.*) Lisa, be quiet at once! I won't allow you to…! (*She breaks away sharply from her. A pause.*)

LISA   (*Slowly, breaking away.*) Oh, yeah! I'm your best friend and you won't allow me! He's got a hold of you too! You're in the grip of that guy and you don't realise it!

JANE   Lisa!

LISA   I pity you! And I pity Charles because he's going to suffer like I'm suffering!

JUANA   (*Gritando.*) ¡Elisa! ¡O callas, o...!

(*Va hacia ella.*)

ELISA   ¡Déjame! ¡Déjame sola con mi pena! Es inútil luchar.
            ¡Es más fuerte que todos! ¡Nos lo está quitando todo!
            ¡Todo! ¡Hasta nuestra amistad! ¡No te reconozco!... ¡No
            te reconozco!...

(*Se va, llorando, por el foro.* JUANA, *agitada y dolida, vacila en seguirla.*
IGNACIO *se levanta.*)

IGNACIO   Juana. (*Ella ahoga un grito y se vuelve hacia* IGNACIO.
            Él llega.) Estaba aquí y os he oído. ¡Pobre Elisa! No le
            guardo rencor.

JUANA   (*Tratando de reprimir su temblor.*) ¿Por qué no
            avisaste?

IGNACIO   No me arrepiento. ¡Juana! (*Le coge una mano.*) Me has
            dado mi primer momento de felicidad. ¡Gracias! ¡Si
            supieras qué hermoso es sentirse comprendido! ¡Qué
            bien has adivinado en mí! Tienes razón. Sufro mucho. Y
            ese sufrimiento me lleva...

JUANA   Ignacio... ¿Por qué no intentas reprimirte? Yo sé muy
            bien que no deseas el mal, pero lo estás haciendo.

IGNACIO   No puedo contenerme. No puedo dejar en la mentira a la
            gente cuando me pregunta... ¡Me horroriza el engaño en
            que viven!

JUANA   ¡Guerra nos has traído y no paz!

IGNACIO   Te lo dije... (*Insinuante.*) En este mismo sitio. Y estoy
            venciendo... Recuerda que tú lo quisiste.

(*Breve pausa.*)

JUANA   ¿Y si yo te pidiera ahora, por tu bien, por el mío y el de
            todos, que te marcharas?

IGNACIO   (*Lento.*) ¿Lo quieres de verdad?

JUANA   (*Con voz muy débil.*) Te lo ruego.

IGNACIO   No. No lo quieres. Tú quieres aliviar mi pena con tu
            dulzura.. ¡Y vas a dármela! ¡Tú me las darás! ¡Tú, que
            me has comprendido y defendido! ¡Te quiero, Juana!

JUANA   ¡Calla!

JANE	(*Shouting.*) Lisa! If you don't shut up, I'll... (*She moves towards her.*)
LISA	Leave me! Leave me alone with my misery! It's pointless struggling. He's stronger than all of us! He's taking everything from us! Everything! Even our friendship! I don't know you any more!... I don't know you![36]... (*She heads off Down-stage, crying.* JANE, *agitated and hurt, hesitates whether or not to follow her.* IGGY *stands up.*)
IGGY	Jane. (*She stifles a cry and turns to* IGGY. *He comes to her.*) I was here all along and I heard you. Poor Lisa! I don't bear her any grudge.
JANE	(*Trying to stop trembling.*) Why didn't you tell us?
IGGY	I'm not sorry I didn't. Jane! (*He takes her hand.*) You've given me my first moment of happiness. Thank you! If you knew how great it is to feel that someone understands! How true it was, what you said about me! You're right. I suffer a lot. And that suffering makes me...
JANE	Iggy... Why don't you try to control yourself? I know full well that you don't want to do wrong, but that's what you're doing.
IGGY	I can't. I can't leave people to their lies when they ask me... The deceit of it all horrifies me!
JANE	You've brought us war, not peace!
IGGY	I told you so... (*Knowingly.*) Right here where we are now. And I'm winning... Remember that you wanted it to be so. (*A brief pause.*)
JANE	And if I were to ask you now, for your sake, for mine and for everyone's, to leave here?
IGGY	(*Slowly.*) Is that what you really want?
JANE	(*With a very faint voice.*) I'm asking you to do it.
IGGY	No. You don't want me to. You want to ease my suffering with your kindness... And you're going to! You will! Yes, you, who've understood and defended me. I love you, Jane!
JANE	Stop!

IGNACIO	Te quiero a ti, y no a ninguna de esas otras. ¡A ti y desde el primer día! Te quiero por tu bondad, por tu encanto, por la ternura de tu voz, por la suavidad de tus manos... (*Transición.*) Te quiero y te necesito. Tú lo sabes.
JUANA	¡Por favor! ¡No debes hablar así! Olvidas que Carlos...
IGNACIO	(*Irónico.*) ¿Carlos? Carlos es un tonto que te dejaría por una vidente. Él cree que nuestro mundo y el de ellos es el mismo... Él querría otra doña Pepita. Otra fea doña Pepita que mirase por él... Desearía una mujer completa, y a ti te tiene como un mal menor. (*Transición.*) ¡Pero yo no quiero una mujer, sino una ciega! ¡Una ciega de mi mundo de ciegos, que comprenda!... Tú. Porque tú sólo puedes amar a un ciego verdadero, no a un pobre iluso que se cree normal. ¡Es a mí a quien amas! No te atreves a decírmelo, ni a confesártelo... Serías la excepción. No te atreves a decir «te quiero». Pero yo lo diré por ti. Sí, me quieres; lo estás adivinando ahora mismo. Lo delata la emoción de tu voz. ¡Me quieres con mi angustia y mi tristeza, para sufrir conmigo de cara a la verdad y de espaldas a todas las mentiras que pretenden enmascarar nuestra desgracia! ¡Porque eres fuerte para eso y porque eres buena!

(*La abraza apasionadamente.*)

JUANA	(*Sofocada.*) ¡No!

(IGNACIO *le sella la boca con un beso prolongado.* JUANA *apenas resiste. Por la derecha han entrado* DON PABLO *y* CARLOS. *Se detienen, sorprendidos.*)

DON PABLO	¿Eh?

(IGNACIO *se separa bruscamente, sin soltar a* JUANA. *Los dos escuchan, agitadísimos.*)

CARLOS	Ha sonado un beso...

(JUANA *se retuerce las manos.*)

DON PABLO	(*Jovial.*) ¡Qué falta de formalidad! ¿Quiénes son los tortolitos que se arrullan por aquí? ¡Tendré que amonestarlos! (*Nadie responde. Demudada,* JUANA

IGGY   I love you, you, and not any of those others. It's been you
                    – since the very first day! I love you for your goodness,
                    your charm, your gentle voice, your soft hands…
                    (*Changing his manner.*) I love you and need you. You
                    know that.[37]

JANE   Please! You mustn't talk like that. You're forgetting that
                    Charles…

IGGY   (*Sarcastically.*) Charles? Charles is a fool who'd leave
                    you for a seer. He thinks our world and theirs are the
                    same… He'd like another Mrs P. Another ugly Mrs P.
                    who'd look out for him… He'd like a whole woman,
                    and he sees you as second best. (*Changing his manner.*)
                    But I don't want a woman, I want a blind woman! A
                    blind woman who belongs to my world of blind people,
                    who understands… That's you. Because you could only
                    love a real blind man, not a poor dreamer who thinks
                    he's normal. It's me you love! You daren't tell me, or
                    even admit it to yourself… Who would? You daren't say
                    "I love you". But I'll say it for you. Yes, you do love me;
                    you're sensing it right now. The trembling in your voice
                    gives it away. You love me, anguish, sadness and all,
                    enough to share my suffering, facing up to the truth and
                    turning our backs on all the lies designed to conceal our
                    misfortune. Because you're strong and because you're
                    good! (*He embraces her passionately.*)

JANE   (*Struggling for breath.*) No! (IGGY *seals her lips with
                    a long kiss.* JANE *scarcely resists.* MR P. *and* CHARLES
                    have entered from the Left. They stop in surprise.)

MR P.   What's that? (IGGY *breaks off sharply, without letting go
                    of* JANE. *The two of them listen, extremely agitated.*)

CHARLES   That was the sound of a kiss… (JANE *wrings her
                    hands.*)

MR P.   (*Jovially.*) How improper! Who are these love-birds
                    cooing around here? I'll have to give them a telling off!
                    (*There is no reply. Her whole demeanour changed,* JANE

vacila en romper a hablar. IGNACIO *le aprieta con fuerza el brazo.*) ¿No contestáis? (IGNACIO, *con el bastón levantado del suelo, conduce rápidamente a* JUANA *hacia la portalada. Sus pasos no titubean; todo él parece estar poseído de una nueva y triunfante seguridad. Ella levanta y baja la cabeza, llena de congoja. Convulsa y medio arrastrada, casi corriendo, se la ve pasar tras* IGNACIO, *que no la suelta, a través de la cristalera del foro.* DON PABLO, *jocosamente:*) ¡Se han marchado! Les dio vergüenza.

CARLOS   (*Serio.*) Sí.

TELÓN

hesitates whether or not to start speaking. IGGY *squeezes her arm tightly.*) Are you not answering? (IGGY, *with his stick up off the ground, leads* JANE *quickly to the doorway. There is no hesitation in his step; he seems entirely possessed by a new, triumphant assurance. Full of anguish, she raises and lowers her head. Convulsed, half-dragged, almost running, she is seen following* IGGY, *who does not let go of her, through the French windows Up-stage.* MR P., *humorously:*) They've gone. They were ashamed.

CHARLES (*Seriously.*) Yes.[38]

CURTAIN

ACTO TERCERO

Saloncito en la Residencia. Amplio ventanal al fondo, con la cortina descorrida, tras el que resplandece la noche estrellada. Haciendo chaflán a la derecha, cortina que oculta una puerta. En el chaflán de la izquierda, un espléndido aparato de radio. En lugar apropiado, estantería con juegos diversos y libros para ciegos. Algún cacharro con flores. En el primer término izquierdo, puerta con su cortina. En el primer término y hacia la derecha, velador de ajedrez con las fichas colocadas, y dos sillas. Bajo el ventanal y hacia el centro de la escena, sofá. Cerca de la radio, una mesa con una lámpara portátil apagada. Sillones, veladores. Encendida la luz central.

(ELISA, *sentada a la derecha del sofá, llora amargamente.* CARLOS *está sentado junto al ajedrez, jugando consigo mismo una partida, con la que intenta distraer su preocupación. Lleva la camisa desabrochada y la corbata floja.*)

ELISA	¡Somos muy desgraciados, Carlos! ¡Muy desgraciados! ¿Por qué nos enamoraremos? Quisiera saberlo. (*Breve pausa.*) Ahora comprendo que no me quería.
CARLOS	Te quería y te quiere. Es Ignacio el culpable de todo. Miguelín es muy joven. Sólo tiene diecisiete años y...
ELISA	¿Verdad? Si yo misma quiero convencerme de que Miguelín volverá... ¡Pero lo dudo, Carlos, lo dudo horriblemente! (*Llora de nuevo. Se calma.*) ¡Qué egoísta soy! También tú sufres, y yo no reparo en hacerte mi paño de lágrimas.

(*Se levanta para ir a su lado.*)

CARLOS	Yo no sufro.
ELISA	Sí sufres, sí... Sufres por Juana. (*Movimiento de* CARLOS.) ¡Por esa grandísima coqueta!
CARLOS	¡Ojalá fuese coquetería!
ELISA	¿Y dices que no sufres? (CARLOS *oculta la cabeza entre las manos.*) ¡Pobre! Ignacio nos ha destrozado a los dos.

ACT III

A small lounge in the students' residence. There is a large window Up-stage, with its curtains drawn back, behind which shines the star-lit night. On the Left is a curtained doorway. In a nook on the Right there is a splendid music system. In a suitable place there are bookshelves lined with a variety of games and books for the blind. Here and there are flowerpots. Down Right is a door with a curtain. Down Left are a chess table with its pieces in place, and two chairs. Beneath the large window and towards the Centre is a sofa. Near to the music system is a table with a portable lamp, switched off. Armchairs and pedestal tables. The central light is on.

(LISA, *sitting on the left of the sofa, is crying bitterly.* CHARLES *is sitting by the chessboard, playing a game by himself, in an attempt to take his mind off his worries. The top button of his shirt is undone and is tie is sloppily worn.*)[39]

LISA	We're a miserable pair, Charles! Very miserable! Why do we fall in love? That's what I want to know. (*A brief pause.*) Now I understand that he didn't love me.
CHARLES	He did love you and he still does. Iggy's to blame for everything. Mikey's very young. He's only seventeen and...
LISA	Do you think so? I really want to convince myself that Mikey'll come back to me... But I doubt it, Charles, I really doubt it! (*She cries again, then calms herself.*) God, I'm terribly selfish! You're suffering too and here I am blubbering on at you. (*She gets up to go over to him.*)
CHARLES	I'm not suffering.
LISA	Yes, you are, yes, you are... you're suffering over Jane. (CHARLES *moves.*) Over that big flirt!
CHARLES	I wish it was just flirting.
LISA	And you say you're not suffering? (CHARLES *buries his head in his hands.*) You poor thing! Iggy has destroyed both of us.

CARLOS	A mí no me ha destrozado nadie.
ELISA	No finjas conmigo... Comprendo muy bien tu pena, porque es como la mía. Te destroza el abandono de Juana y te duele aún más, como a mí, la falta de una explicación definitiva... ¡Es espantoso! Parece que nada ha pasado, y los dos sabemos en nuestro corazón que todo se ha perdido.
CARLOS	(*Con ímpetu.*) ¡No se ha perdido nada! ¡No puede perderse nada! Me niego a sufrir.
ELISA	¡Me asustas!
CARLOS	Sí. Me niego a sufrir. ¿Dices que soy desgraciado? ¡Es mentira! ¿Que sufro por Juana? No puedo sufrir por ella porque no ha dejado de quererme. ¿Entiendes? ¡No ha dejado de quererme! Tiene que ser así y es así.
ELISA	(*Compadecida.*) ¡Pobre!... ¡Qué dolor el tuyo..., y sin lágrimas! ¡Llora, llora como yo! ¡Desahógate!
CARLOS	(*Tenaz.*) Me niego a llorar. ¡Llora tú si quieres! Pero harás mal. Tampoco tienes motivo. ¡No debes tenerlo! Miguelín te quiere y volverá a ti. Juana no ha dejado de quererme.
ELISA	Me explico tu falta de valor para reconocer los hechos... Yo también he querido – ¡y aún quiero a veces! – engañarme, pero...
CARLOS	(*En el colmo de la desesperación.*) Pero ¿no comprendes que no podemos dejarnos vencer por Ignacio? ¡Si sufrimos por su culpa, ese sufrimiento será para él una victoria! Y no debemos darle ninguna. ¡Ninguna!
ELISA	(*Asustada.*) Pero en la intimidad podemos alguna vez compadecernos mutuamente...
CARLOS	Ni en la intimidad siquiera.

(*Pausa. Poco a poco, inclina de nuevo la cabeza.* JUANA *entra por la puerta del chaflán.*)

JUANA	¿Ignacio? (ELISA *abre la boca.* CARLOS *le aprieta el brazo para que calle.*) Tampoco está aquí. Dónde estará el pobre...

(*Avanza hacia el lateral izquierdo y desaparece por la puerta.*)

CHARLES	Nobody's destroyed me.
LISA	Don't bluff me... I understand your pain very well, because it's like mine. Jane's leaving you is destroying you and what hurts even more, for me too, is the lack of a clear explanation... It's dreadful! It seems like nothing's happened, but we both know deep down that all's lost.
CHARLES	(*Forcefully.*) Nothing's been lost! Nothing can be lost! I refuse to suffer.
LISA	You're frightening me!
CHARLES	Well, I refuse to suffer. You say I'm miserable? That's a lie! That I'm suffering over Jane? I can't suffer over her because she hasn't stopped loving me. Do you understand? She hasn't stopped loving me! It has to be like that, and that's the way it is.
LISA	(*Moved.*) Poor thing!... That's some pain you have... and no tears! Cry, cry like me! Get it out of your system!
CHARLES	(*Doggedly.*) I refuse to cry. Cry if you want! But it's not a good thing. You've no reason to. You can't have! Mikey loves you and he'll be back with you. Jane hasn't stopped loving me.
LISA	I can understand that you can't face up to facts... Me too, I've wanted – and still sometimes do – to fool myself but...
CHARLES	(*At the height of despair.*) But, don't you understand that we can't allow ourselves to be beaten by Iggy? If we suffer on his account, that suffering'll be a victory for him. And we mustn't give him a sniff of victory. Not a sniff!
LISA	(*Frightened.*) But sometimes we can take pity on each other in private...
CHARLES	Not even in private. (*A pause. Gradually he lowers his head again.* JANE *enters by the curtained doorway.*)
JANE	Iggy? (LISA *is about to speak.* CHARLES *squeezes her arm to keep her quiet.*) Not here either. Where could the poor fellow be... (*She moves Down Right and disappears through the door.*)

ELISA	(*Emocionada.*) ¡Carlos!
CARLOS	Calla.
ELISA	¡Oh! ¿Qué te pasa? No estás normal... Yo no hubiera podido resistirlo.
CARLOS	(*Casi sonriente.*) Si no ocurre nada, mujer... Otra... Otra que busca al pobre Ignacio, que le llama por las habitaciones... Nada.
ELISA	No te entiendo. No sé si estás desesperado o loco.
CARLOS	Ninguna de las dos cosas. Nunca tuve el juicio más claro que ahora. (*Le da palmaditas en la mano.*) ¡Anímate, Elisa! Todo se arreglará.

(*Entran por el chaflán* IGNACIO *y* MIGUELÍN, *charlando con animación.* ELISA *se oprime las manos al oírlos.*)

IGNACIO	No todas las mujeres son iguales, aunque es indudable que las ciegas se llevan muy poco entre ellas..., con alguna excepción. Conocí una vez a una muchacha vidente...
MIGUEL	(*Interrumpe, impulsivo.*) Son muy simpáticas las chicas videntes. Yo conozco a una que se llama Carmen y que era mi vecina. Yo no le hacía caso, pero ella estaba por mí...
IGNACIO	¿Sabes si era fea?
MIGUEL	(*Cortado.*) Pues... no... No llegué a enterarme.
CARLOS	Buenas noches, amigos. ¿No os sentáis?
MIGUEL	(*Inmutado.*) ¡Hombre, Carlos, tengo ganas de hablar contigo! No sé cómo me las arreglo que nunca encuentro la manera de charlar contigo. Ni con Elisa.
ELISA	(*Con esfuerzo.*) Estás a tiempo.
MIGUEL	(*Con desgana.*) ¡Caramba!, si está Elisa contigo. Y ¿cómo te va, Elisa?
ELISA	(*Seca.*) Bien, gracias.
MIGUEL	(*Trivial.*) ¡Vaya! Me alegro.
CARLOS	(*Articulando con mucha claridad.*) Creo que Juanita andaba por ahí buscándote, Ignacio.

(ELISA *se queda sobrecogida.*)

LISA	(*Overcome.*) Charles!
CHARLES	Be quiet.
LISA	Oh, what's happening to you? You're not your usual self… I couldn't have resisted.
CHARLES	(*Almost smiling.*) I tell you, it's no big deal, … Just another girl… another girl looking for poor Iggy, calling him from room to room… No big deal at all.
LISA	I don't understand you. I don't know if you're desperate or mad.
CHARLES	Neither. My judgement's never been clearer. (*He pats her hand gently.*) Come on, Lisa! Everything'll be sorted.[40] (IGGY *and* MIKEY *enter by the curtained doorway, chatting animatedly. On hearing them,* LISA *wrings her hands.*)
IGGY	Not all women are the same, although there's no doubt that blind women are mostly quite alike… with some exceptions. I once knew a girl who was a seer…
MIKEY	(*Interrupts, impulsively.*) Girls who are seers are very nice. I know one called Carol who was my neighbour. I didn't pay her any heed, but she was keen on me…
IGGY	Do you know if she was ugly?
MIKEY	(*Stunned.*) Well… no… I didn't find out.
CHARLES	'Evening, lads. Won't you sit down?
MIKEY	(*Perturbed.*) Hey, Charles, I really want to talk to you! I don't know how I manage, but I never seem to be able to get to talk to you, or Lisa.
LISA	(*Making an effort.*) Here's your chance now.
MIKEY	(*Half-heartedly.*) Gosh, and Lisa's with you! And, how are things, Lisa?
LISA	(*Drily.*) Fine, thanks.
MIKEY	(*Nonchalantly.*) Oh, well, I'm delighted.
CHARLES	(*Articulating very clearly.*) I think Jane was round and about looking for you, Iggy. (LISA *is stunned.*)

IGNACIO	(*Turbado.*) No... No sé...
CARLOS	Sí. Sí. Te buscaba.
IGNACIO	(*Repuesto.*) Es posible. Teníamos que hablar de algunas cosas.
MIGUEL	Oye, Ignacio. Creo que podrías seguir hablando de esa muchacha vidente a quien conociste. Elisa y Carlos no tendrán inconveniente.
CARLOS	Ninguno.
IGNACIO	A Carlos y a Elisa no les interesan estos temas. Son muy abstractos.
CARLOS	Creo que una muchacha de carne y hueso no es nada abstracta.
IGNACIO	Pero ve. ¿Quieres más abstracción para nosotros?
ELISA	(*Con violencia.*) Me disculparéis, pero Ignacio tiene razón: no puedo soportar esos temas. Me voy a acostar.
CARLOS	A tu gusto. Perdona que no te acompañe; quisiera continuar charlando con Ignacio. Miguelín te acompañará.

(MIGUELÍN *acoge con desagrado la indicación.*)

ELISA	(*Agria.*) Que no se moleste por mí. Miguelín quiere seguramente seguir hablando contigo... y con Ignacio.
MIGUEL	(*Sin pizca de alegría.*) Qué tonterías dices... Te acompañaré con mucho gusto.
ELISA	Como quieras. Buenas noches a los dos.
IGNACIO	Buenas noches.
CARLOS	Hasta mañana, Elisa.

(ELISA *se va por la izquierda.* MIGUELÍN *la sigue como un perro apaleado.* CARLOS *e* IGNACIO *se acomodan en dos sillones de la izquierda, pero antes de que comiencen a hablar entra por el chaflán* DOÑA PEPITA.)

DOÑA PEPITA	¡Buenas noches! ¿No se acuestan ustedes?

(CARLOS *e* IGNACIO *se levantan.*)

CARLOS	Es pronto.
DOÑA PEPITA	Siéntense, por favor. Y usted, hombre del bastón, ¿no dice nada?
IGNACIO	Buenas noches.

IGGY	(*Confused.*) No... I don't know...[41]
CHARLES	Yeah, yeah. She was looking for you.
IGGY	(*His poise recovered.*) That's possible. We had to talk about a few things.
MIKEY	Listen, Iggy. I think you could carry on talking about that girl you knew who was a seer. Lisa and Charles wouldn't mind.
CHARLES	Not at all.
IGGY	Charles and Lisa aren't interested in those matters. They're very abstract things.
CHARLES	I think that a real flesh and blood girl isn't abstract at all.
IGGY	But she can see. What could be more abstract than that for us?
LISA	(*Forcefully.*) You'll excuse me, but Iggy's right; I can't stand talking about this. I'm off to bed.
CHARLES	As you wish. Sorry I'm not seeing you back to your room; I want to continue talking to Iggy. Mikey'll go along with you. (MIKEY *reluctantly takes the hint.*)
LISA	(*Bitterly.*) Don't let him put himself out for me. Mikey'll surely want to carry on talking to you... and Iggy.
MIKEY	(*Not at all happy.*) Nonsense... I'll go along with you, with great pleasure.
LISA	As you wish. Good night to both of you.
IGGY	Good night.
CHARLES	See you tomorrow, Lisa. (LISA *heads off Right.* MIKEY *follows her like a submissive dog.* CHARLES *and* IGGY *settle into two armchairs on the Right, but before they start talking,* MRS P. *comes in from the curtained doorway.*)
MRS P.	Good evening. Not going to bed? (CHARLES *and* IGGY *get up.*)
CHARLES	It's early.
MRS P.	Please sit down. And you, with your stick, what have you got to say for yourself?
IGGY	Good evening.

DOÑA PEPITA	¡Alégrese, hombre! Le encuentro cada día más mustio. Bueno, prosigan su charla. Yo voy a dar una vuelta por los dormitorios. Hasta ahora.
CARLOS	Adiós, doña Pepita.

(DOÑA PEPITA *se va por la izquierda. Pausa.*)

IGNACIO	Supongo que si quieres quedarte conmigo no será para hablar de la muchacha vidente.
CARLOS	Supones bien.
IGNACIO	Me has hablado varias veces y siempre del mismo tema. ¿También es hoy del mismo tema?
CARLOS	También.
IGNACIO	Paciencia. ¿Podrías decirme si tendremos que hablar muchas veces todavía de lo mismo?
CARLOS	Creo que serán pocas... Quizá ésta sea la última.
IGNACIO	Me alegro. Puedes empezar cuando quieras.
CARLOS	Ignacio... El día en que viniste aquí quisiste marcharte al poco rato. (*Con amargura.*) Lo supe en la época en que Juana aún me hacía confidencias. Tuviste entonces una buena idea, y creo que es el momento de ponerla en práctica. ¡Márchate!
IGNACIO	Parece una orden...
CARLOS	Cuya conveniencia estoy dispuesto a explicarte.
IGNACIO	Te envía don Pablo, ¿verdad?
CARLOS	No. Pero debes irte.
IGNACIO	¿Por qué?
CARLOS	Debes irte porque tu influencia está pesando demasiado sobre esta casa. Y tu influencia es destructora. Si no te vas, esta casa se hundirá. ¡Pero antes de que eso ocurra tú te habrás ido!
IGNACIO	Palabrería. No pienso marcharme, naturalmente. Ya sé que algunos lo deseáis. Empezando por don Pablo. Pero él no se atreve a decirme nada, porque no hay motivo para ello. ¿De verdad no me hablas... en su nombre?
CARLOS	Es el interés del centro el que me mueve a hablarte.
IGNACIO	Más palabrería. ¡Qué aficionado eres a los tópicos! Pues escúchame. Estoy seguro de que la mayoría de los compañeros desea mi permanencia. Por lo tanto, no me voy.

MRS P.	Cheer up, man! Every day you're more down in the mouth. Ok, carry on with your chat. I'm going to take a walk round the dorms. See you soon.
CHARLES	Bye, Mrs P. (MRS P. *heads off Right. A pause.*)
IGGY	I guess if you want to stay with me it's not to talk about the girl who was a seer.
CHARLES	You're right.
IGGY	You've spoken to me several times and it's always about the same thing. Is it that again this evening?
CHARLES	Yes.
IGGY	Steady on. Can you tell me if we still have to talk on many more occasions about the same thing?
CHARLES	Not many. I think… This might be the last.[42]
IGGY	I'm delighted. You can start when you want.
CHARLES	Iggy… The day you came here you wanted to leave in no time. (*Bitterly.*) I found that out in the days when Jane still confided in me. You had a good idea back then, and I think this is the time to put it into practice. Leave!
IGGY	Seems like an order…
CHARLES	I'm willing to explain it to you.
IGGY	Mr P.'s sent you, hasn't he?
CHARLES	No. But you must leave.
IGGY	Why?
CHARLES	You must leave because your influence is weighing too heavily on this place. And your influence is destructive. If you don't go, the place'll fall apart. But before that happens, you'll have left!
IGGY	That's just talk. I've no intention of going, of course. I know that some of you want me to. Mr P., for starters. But he doesn't dare to say a word to me, because there's no good reason for it. Truthfully now, you're not speaking on his behalf?
CHARLES	It's the interest of the Centre as a whole that's making me speak to you.
IGGY	More talk. You love your little trite phrases! Well, listen to me. I'm sure that the majority of our fellow students want me to stay. So, I'm not going.

CARLOS ¡   Qué te importan a ti los compañeros!

(*Breve pausa.*)

IGNACIO   El mayor obstáculo que hay entre tú y yo está en que
                no me comprendes. (*Ardientemente.*) ¡Los compañeros,
                y tú con ellos, me interesáis más de lo que crees! Me
                duele como una mutilación propia vuestra ceguera;
                ¡me duele, a mí, por todos vosotros! (*Con arrebato.*)
                ¡Escucha! ¿No te has dado cuenta al pasar por la terraza
                de que la noche estaba seca y fría? ¿No sabes lo que eso
                significa? No lo sabes, claro. Pues eso quiere decir que
                ahora están brillando las estrellas con todo su esplendor,
                y que los videntes gozan de la maravilla de su presencia.
                Esos mundos lejanísimos están ahí (*Se ha acercado
                al ventanal y toca los cristales.*)*,* tras los cristales, al
                alcance de nuestra vista..., ¡si la tuviéramos! (*Breve
                pausa.*) A ti eso no te importa, desdichado. Pues yo las
                añoro, quisiera contemplarlas; siento gravitar su dulce
                luz sobre mi rostro, ¡y me parece que casi las veo! (*Vuelto
                extáticamente hacia el ventanal.* CARLOS *se vuelve un
                poco, sugestionado a su pesar.*) Bien sé que si gozara de
                la vista moriría de pesar por no poder alcanzarlas. ¡Pero
                al menos las vería! Y ninguno de nosotros las ve, Carlos.
                ¿Y crees malas estas preocupaciones? Tú sabes que no
                pueden serlo. ¡Es imposible que tú – por poco que sea
                – no las sientas también!
CARLOS   (*Tenaz.*) ¡No! Yo no las siento.
IGNACIO   No las sientes, ¿eh? Y ésa es tu desgracia: no sentir la
                esperanza que yo os he traído.
CARLOS   ¿Qué esperanza?
IGNACIO   La esperanza de la luz.
CARLOS   ¿De la luz?
IGNACIO   ¡De la luz, sí! Porque nos dicen incurables; pero ¿qué
                sabemos nosotros de eso? Nadie sabe lo que el mundo
                puede reservarnos; desde el descubrimiento científico...
                hasta el milagro.
CARLOS   (*Despectivo.*) ¡Ah, bah!

CHARLES   What do you care about your fellow students? (*A brief pause.*)

IGGY   The biggest obstacle between you and me is that you don't understand me. (*Passionately.*) My fellow students, and you among them, interest me more than you think! The blindness of all of you pains me like a wound to myself; it pains me what's happening to all of you! (*Angrily.*) Listen! Didn't you notice when you were out on the terrace that the night was dry and cold? Don't you know what that means? You don't, of course. Well that means that right now the stars are shining in all their splendour, and that seers are enjoying the wonder of their presence. Those very distant worlds are there (*He has moved to the large window and touches the pane.*), beyond this glass, within range of our sight..., if we had sight! (*A brief pause.*) That doesn't matter to you, you miserable wretch. Well, I long for the stars, I want to contemplate them; I feel their sweet light on my face, and it seems to me that I can almost see them! (*He has turned in ecstasy towards the large window.* CHARLES *turns around slightly, affected by* IGGY*'s sorrow.*) I know full well that if I had sight I'd die of a broken heart over not being able to reach them. But at least I'd see them! And none of us can see them, Charles. And you think these worries are wrong? You know they can't be. It's inconceivable that you – even in some small way – don't share them![43]

CHARLES   (*Tenaciously.*) No! No, I don't.

IGGY   You don't, eh? That's your misfortune: not sensing the hope I've brought you all.

CHARLES   What hope?

IGGY   The hope of light.[44]

CHARLES   Light?

IGGY   Yes, light. Because it's said we're incurable; but, what do we know about that? No one knows what the world might have in store for us; from scientific discovery... through to miracles.

CHARLES   (*Contemptuously.*) Bah!

IGNACIO	Ya, ya sé que tú lo rechazas. ¡Rechazas la fe que te traigo!
CARLOS	¡Basta! Luz, visión... Palabras vacías. ¡Nosotros estamos ciegos! ¿Entiendes?
IGNACIO	Menos mal que lo reconoces... Creí que sólo éramos... invidentes.
CARLOS	¡Ciegos, sí! Sea.
IGNACIO	¿Ciegos de qué?
CARLOS	(*Vacilante.*) ¿De qué?...
IGNACIO	¡De la luz! De algo que anhelas comprender... aunque lo niegues. (*Transición.*) Escucha: yo sé muchas cosas. Yo sé que los videntes tratan a veces de imaginarse nuestra desgracia, y para ello cierran los ojos. (*La luz del escenario empieza a bajar.*) Entonces se estremecen de horror. Alguno de ellos enloqueció, creyéndose ciego..., porque no abrieron al tiempo la ventana de su cuarto. (*El escenario está oscuro. Sólo las estrellas brillan en la ventana.*) ¡Pues en ese horror y en esa locura estamos sumidos nosotros!... ¡Sin saber lo que es! (*Las estrellas comienzan a apagarse.*) Y por eso es para mí doblemente espantoso. (*Oscuridad absoluta en el escenario y en el teatro.*) Nuestras voces se cruzan... en la tiniebla.
CARLOS	(*Con ligera aprensión en la voz.*) ¡Ignacio!
IGNACIO	Sí. Es una palabra terrible por lo misteriosa. Empiezas..., empiezas a comprender. (*Breve pausa.*) Yo he sentido cómo los videntes se alegran cuando vuelve la luz por la mañana. (*Las estrellas comienzan a lucir de nuevo, al tiempo que empieza a iluminarse otra vez el escenario.*) Van identificando los objetos, gozándose en sus formas y sus... colores. ¡Se saturan de la alegría de la luz, que es para ellos como un verdadero don de Dios! Un don tan grande, que se ingeniaron para producirlo de noche. Pero para nosotros todo es igual. La luz puede volver; puede ir sacando de la oscuridad las formas y los colores; puede dar a las cosas su plenitud de existencia. (*La luz del escenario y de las estrellas ha vuelto del todo.*) ¡Incluso a las lejanas estrellas! ¡Es igual! Nada vemos.

IGGY	I know you reject all this. You reject the faith I bring you!
CHARLES	That's enough! Light, vision... empty words. We're blind! Do you understand?
IGGY	Good thing you recognise that... I thought we were only... non-seers.
CHARLES	Blind, ok! Whatever.
IGGY	Blind to what?
CHARLES	(*Hesitantly.*) To what...?
IGGY	To light! To something that you yearn to understand... even though you deny it. (*Changes his manner.*) Listen: I know a lot of stuff. I know that seers try sometimes to imagine our misfortune, and that to do that, they close their eyes. (*The stage lighting begins to dim.*) Then they shudder in horror. The odd one of them goes mad, thinking he's blind..., because the window of his room isn't opened on time. (*The stage is dark. Only the stars shine, through the window.*) Well, we find ourselves plunged into that sort of horror and madness!... Without knowing what it is! (*The light of the stars begins to go out.*) And, to my way of thinking, that's what makes it twice as awful. (*Complete darkness on stage and in the theatre.*) Our voices crisscross... in the darkness.[45]
CHARLES	(*With a slightly apprehensive voice.*) Iggy!
IGGY	Yes. It's a terrible word, so mysterious. You begin..., you begin to understand. (*A brief pause.*) I've sensed how seers are so happy when light is restored at morning-time. (*The stars begin to shine once more just as the stage starts being lit up again.*) They gradually identify objects, appreciating their shapes and their... colours. They luxuriate in the joy of light which, to them, is like a real gift from God! So great a gift that people strove to reproduce it at night-time. But for us everything's the same. Light can return; it can pluck shapes and colours from darkness, it can imbue things with the fullness of existence. (*The light on-stage and from the stars has been fully restored.*) Even the distant stars! It's all the same to us! We can see nothing.

CARLOS   (*Sacudiendo con brusquedad la involuntaria influencia sufrida a causa de las palabras de* IGNACIO.) ¡Cállate! Te comprendo, sí, te comprendo; pero no te puedo disculpar. (*Con el acento del que percibe una revelación súbita.*) Eres... ¡un mesiánico desequilibrado! Yo te explicaré lo que te pasa: tienes el instinto de la muerte. Dices que quieres ver... ¡Lo que quieres es morir!

IGNACIO   Quizá... Quizá. Puede que la muerte sea la única forma de conseguir la definitiva visión...

CARLOS   O la oscuridad definitiva. Pero es igual. Morir es lo que buscas, y no lo sabes. Morir y hacer morir a los demás. Por eso debes marcharte. ¡Yo defiendo la vida! ¡La vida de todos nosotros, que tú amenazas! Porque quiero vivirla a fondo, cumplirla; aunque no sea pacífica ni feliz. Aunque sea dura y amarga. ¡Pero la vida sabe a algo, nos pide algo, nos reclama! (*Pausa breve.*) Todos luchábamos por la vida aquí... hasta que tú viniste. ¡Márchate!

IGNACIO   Buen abogado de la vida eres. No me sorprende. La vida te rebosa. Hablas así y quieres que me vaya por una razón bien vital: ¡Juana!

(*Por la izquierda aparece* DOÑA PEPITA, *que los observa.*)

CARLOS   (*Levanta los puños amenazantes.*) ¡Ignacio!

DOÑA PEPITA   (*Rápida.*) ¿Todavía aquí? Se ve que la charla es interesante. (CARLOS *baja los brazos.*) Parece como si estuviera usted representando, querido Carlos.

CARLOS   (*Reportándose.*) Casi, casi, doña Pepita.

DOÑA PEPITA   (*Cruzando.*) Váyanse a acostar y será mejor. Don Pablo y yo vendremos ahora a trabajar un rato. Buenas noches.

CARLOS e IGNACIO   Buenas noches.

(DOÑA PEPITA *se vuelve y los mira con gesto dubitativo desde el chaflán. Después se va.*)

CARLOS   (*Sereno.*) Has pronunciado el nombre de Juana. Juana no tiene ninguna relación con esto. Prescindamos de ella.

IGNACIO   ¡Cómo! ¡Me la citas dos veces y dices ahora que es asunto

CHARLES   (*Brusquely shaking off the involuntary influence caused by* IGGY*'s words*.) Be quiet! I understand you, yes, I understand; but I can't excuse you. (*Said as though he had just had a sudden revelation*.) You're... a half-mad Messiah! I'll explain what's happening to you: you've a death wish. You say you want to see... What you want is to die!

IGGY   Maybe... maybe. Perhaps death is the only way of achieving definitive vision...[46]

CHARLES   Or definitive darkness. Whatever. Dying is what you're after, and you don't know it. Dying and making others die. That's why you must leave. I defend life! The life that we all have, that's threatened by you! Because I want to live it to the full, to see it through; even if it isn't peaceful or happy. Even if it's hard and bitter. But life has its own flavour, it asks things of us, it makes demands on us! (*A brief pause*.) We were all struggling for life here... until you showed up. Leave!

IGGY   You're a good advocate for life. That doesn't surprise me. You're bursting with life. You talk like that and you want me to go for one absolutely vital reason: Jane! (*To the Right appears* MRS P. *who watches them*.)

CHARLES   (*Raises his fists menacingly*.) Iggy!

MRS P.   (*Quickly*.) Still here? Evidently the chat's interesting. (CHARLES *lowers his arms*.) It looks like you were playing a part, Charles dear.

CHARLES   (*Pulling himself together*.) Nearly, Mrs P., nearly.

MRS P.   (*Crossing the stage*.) It'd be best if you went off to bed. Mr P. and I are coming here to work for a while now. Good night.

CHARLES & IGGY   Good night. (MRS P. *turns and looks dubiously at them from the curtained doorway. Then she exits*.)

CHARLES   (*Calmly*.) You mentioned Jane's name. Jane has nothing to do with this. Let's leave her out of it.

IGGY   What? You refer to her twice and now you say she's

aparte! No te creía tan hipócrita. Juana es la razón de tu furia, amigo mío...

CARLOS   No estoy furioso.

IGNACIO   Pues de tu disgusto. El recuerdo de Juana es el culpable de ese hermoso canto a la vida que me has brindado.

CARLOS   ¡Te repito que dejemos a Juana! Antes de que... la envenenaras, ya te había hablado yo por primera vez.

IGNACIO   Mientes. Ya entonces no era totalmente tuya, y tú lo presentías. Pues bien: ¡quiero a Juana! Es cierto. Tampoco yo estoy desprovisto de razones vitales. ¡Y por ella no me voy! Como por ella quieres tú que me marche. (*Pausa breve.*) Te daré una alegría momentánea: Juana no es aún totalmente mía.

CARLOS   (*Tranquilo.*) En el fondo de todos los tipos como tú hay siempre lo mismo: baja y cochina lascivia. Ésa es la razón de tu misticismo. No volveré a hablarte de esto. Te marcharás de aquí sea como sea.

IGNACIO   (*Riendo.*) Carlitos, no podrás hacer nada contra mí. No me iré de ningún modo. Y aunque algunas veces pensé en el suicidio, ahora ya no pienso hacerlo.

CARLOS   Esperas, sin duda, a que te dé el ejemplo alguno de los muchachos que has sabido conducir al desaliento.

IGNACIO   (*Cansado.*) No discutamos más. Y dispensa mis ironías. No me agradan, pero tú me provocas demasiado. Lo siento. Y ahora, sí me marcho, pero va a ser al campo de deportes. La noche está muy agradable y quiero cansarme un poco para dormir. (*Serio.*) Las maravillosas estrellas verterán su luz para mí, aunque no las vea. (*Se dirige al chaflán.*) ¿No quieres acompañarme?

CARLOS   No.

IGNACIO   Adiós.

CARLOS   Adiós. (IGNACIO *sale.* CARLOS *se deja caer en una de las sillas del ajedrez y tantea abstraído las piezas. Habla solo, con rabia contenida.*) ¡No, no quiero acompañarte! Nunca te acompañaré a tu infierno. ¡Que lo hagan otros!

not involved! I didn't think you were such a hypocrite. Jane's the reason for your fury, my friend...

CHARLES   I'm not furious.

IGGY   Well, then, for your displeasure. Thinking of Jane has brought on that lovely hymn to life that you performed for me.

CHARLES   I'll say it again, leave Jane out of it! Before... you poisoned her, I had already spoken to you.

IGGY   You're lying. At that stage she wasn't totally yours, and you sensed it. Well, here it is: I love Jane! That's for sure. I'm not without reasons for living either. And it's because of her that I'm not leaving! Just as it's because of her that you want me to leave. (*A brief pause.*) I'll give you a glimpse of happiness, though: Jane still isn't totally mine.

CHARLES   (*Calmly.*) Deep down in guys like you it's always the same thing: base, dirty lust. That's what lies behind your mysticism. I won't talk to you about this matter again. You're leaving here, by whatever means.

IGGY   (*Laughing.*) Charley boy, you'll not be able to do a thing against me. There's no way I'm leaving. And although I sometimes thought of suicide, now I've put that out of my mind.

CHARLES   No doubt you're waiting for one of the guys you've driven to despair to set the example.

IGGY   (*Wearily.*) No more discussion. And sorry about my sarcastic remarks. They're not my style, but you provoke me too much. I'm sorry. Now, I am leaving, but only as far as the sports field. It's a lovely night and I want to unwind a little before bedtime. (*Seriously.*) The marvellous stars will shed their light for me, though I can't see them. (*He moves towards the curtained doorway.*) Do you want to come with me?

CHARLES   No.

IGGY   Goodbye.

CHARLES   Goodbye. (IGGY *exits.* CHARLES *flops into one of the chairs by the chessboard and, lost in thought, fingers the pieces. He speaks alone, with controlled anger.*) No, no I don't want to go with you! I'll never go with you to your hell. Let others go!

(*Momentos después entran por el chaflán* DON PABLO *y* DOÑA PEPITA. *Ésta trae su cartera de cuero.*)

DOÑA PEPITA	¿Aún aquí?
CARLOS	(*Levantando la cabeza.*) Sí, doña Pepita. No tengo sueño.
DON PABLO	(*Que ha sido conducido por* DOÑA PEPITA *al sofá.*) Buenas noches, Carlos.
CARLOS	Buenas noches, don Pablo.
DOÑA PEPITA	(*Curiosa.*) ¿Se fue ya Ignacio a acostar?
CARLOS	Sí... Creo que sí.
DON PABLO	(*Grave.*) Me alegro de encontrarle aquí, Carlos. Quería precisamente hablar con usted de Ignacio. ¿Quieres darme un cigarrillo, Pepita? (DOÑA PEPITA *saca de su cartera un paquete de tabaco y extrae un cigarrillo.*) Sí, Carlos. Creo que esto no es ya una puerilidad. (*A* DOÑA PEPITA, *que le pone el cigarrillo en la boca y se lo enciende.*) Gracias. (DOÑA PEPITA *se sienta a la mesa, saca papeles de la cartera y comienza a anotarlos con la estilográfica.*) La situación a que ha llegado el centro es grave. ¿Usted cree posible que un solo hombre pueda desmoralizar a cien compañeros? Yo no me lo explico.
DOÑA PEPITA	Hay un detalle que aún no sabes... Muchos estudiantes han empezado a descuidar su indumentaria.
DON PABLO	¿Sí?
DOÑA PEPITA	No envían sus trajes a planchar... o prescinden de la corbata, como Ignacio.

(*Pausa breve.* CARLOS *palpa involuntariamente la suya.*)

DON PABLO	Supongo que no dejará de hablar en todo el día. Y aun así, tiene que faltarle tiempo. ¿Usted qué opina, Carlos? (*Pausa.*) ¿Eh?

(DOÑA PEPITA *mira a* CARLOS.)

CARLOS	Perdone. ¿Decía...?
DON PABLO	Que cómo es posible que Ignacio se baste y se sobre para desalentar a tantos invidentes remotos. ¿Qué saben ellos de la luz?

(*Moments later* MR *and* MRS P. *enter by the curtained doorway. She has her leather briefcase.*)[47]

MRS P.	Still here?
CHARLES	(*Raising his head.*) Yes, Mrs P. I'm not tired.
MR P.	(*Who has been led to the sofa by* MRS P.) Good evening, Charles.
CHARLES	Good evening, Mr P.
MRS P.	(*Curiously.*) Has Iggy gone to bed?
CHARLES	Yes… I think so.
MR P.	(*Gravely.*) I'm glad to find you here, Charles. You're the very man I wanted to talk to… about Iggy. Would you give me a cigarette, Fran? (MRS P. *takes a cigarette packet from her briefcase and takes out a cigarette.*) Yes, Charles. I think this is no longer a case of childish behaviour. (*To* MRS P*., who puts the cigarette in his mouth and lights it.*) Thanks. (MRS P. *sits down at the table, takes some papers out of the briefcase and starts making notes with a pen.*) The state of affairs here in the Centre has become serious. Do you think it's possible that one single man could demoralise a hundred fellow students? I can't work it out.
MRS P.	There's a detail you don't know about yet… Many students have started letting their appearance slip.[48]
MR P.	Really?
MRS P.	They don't have their clothes ironed… or don't wear a tie, like Iggy. (*A brief pause.* CHARLES *unwittingly touches his tie.*)
MR P.	I suppose he talks all day. And even at that, he hasn't enough time. What do you think, Charles? (*A pause.*) Eh? (MRS P. *looks at* CHARLES.)
CHARLES	Sorry. You were saying…?
MR P.	Just that how come Iggy is more than capable of disheartening so many simple non-seers? What do they know about light?

| CARLOS | (*Grave.*) Acaso porque la ignoran les preocupe. |
| DON PABLO | (*Sonriente.*) Eso es muy sutil, hijo mío. |

(*Se levanta.*)

CARLOS	Pero es real. Mis desgraciados compañeros sufren la fascinación de todo lo misterioso. ¡Es una pena! Por lo demás, Ignacio no está solo. Él ha lanzado una semilla que ha dado retoños y ahora tiene muchos auxiliares inconscientes. (*Breve pausa. Triste.*) Y los primeros, las muchachas.
DOÑA PEPITA	(*Suave.*) Yo creo que esos retoños carecen de importancia. Si Ignacio, por ejemplo, se marchase, se les iría con él la fuerza moral para continuar su labor negativa.
DON PABLO	Si Ignacio se marchase, todo se arreglaría. Podríamos echarlo, pero... eso sería terrible para el prestigio del centro. ¿No podría usted, por lo pronto, insinuarle a título particular – ¡y con mucha suavidad, desde luego! – la conveniencia de su marcha? (*Pausa.*) ¡Carlos!
CARLOS	Perdón. Estaba distraído. No le he entendido bien...
DOÑA PEPITA	Está usted muy raro esta noche. Don Pablo le decía que si no podría usted sugerirle a Ignacio que se marchase.
DON PABLO	Salvo que tenga alguna idea mejor...

(*Breve pausa.*)

CARLOS	He hablado ya con él.
DON PABLO	¿Sí? ¿Y qué?
CARLOS	Nada. Dice que no se irá.
DON PABLO	Le hablaría cordialmente, con todo el tacto necesario...
CARLOS	Del modo más adecuado. No se preocupe por eso.
DON PABLO	¿Y por qué no quiere irse?

(*Pausa.* DOÑA PEPITA *mira curiosamente a* CARLOS.)

CARLOS	No lo sé.
DON PABLO	¡Pues de un modo u otro tendrá que irse!
CARLOS	Sí. Tiene que irse.
DON PABLO	(*Con aire preocupado.*) Tiene que irse. Es el enemigo más desconcertante que ha tenido nuestra obra hasta

CHARLES	(*Seriously.*) Perhaps it worries them because they don't know about it.
MR P.	(*Smiling.*) That's very subtle, lad. (*He gets up.*)
CHARLES	But it's true. My poor fellow students are afflicted by a fascination with anything mysterious. It's a pity! On top of that, Iggy isn't alone. He's cast a seed that's had many shoots and now he has many unwitting helpers. (*A brief pause. Sadly.*) Top of the list, the girls.
MR P.	(*Softly.*) I think those shoots are not important. If Iggy, for instance, were to leave, their moral strength to carry on the negative work would disappear with him.
MR P.	If Iggy left, everything would be settled. We could expel him, but… that would be awful for the Centre's prestige. Couldn't you, for now, in a private capacity – with great delicacy, of course! – drop him a hint about how convenient it'd be if he left? (*A pause.*) Charles?
CHARLES	Sorry. I was distracted. I didn't quite catch what you were saying…
MRS P.	You're in funny form tonight. Mr P. was saying that you might suggest to Iggy that he leaves.
MR P.	Unless you have a better idea… (*A brief pause.*)
CHARLES	I've already spoken to him.
MR P.	Yes, and…?
CHARLES	And nothing. He says he won't go.
MR P.	You'd have talked to him nicely, with all due tact…
CHARLES	In the best possible way. Don't worry about that.
MR P.	And why doesn't he want to go? (*A pause.* MRS P. *looks inquisitively at* CHARLES.)
CHARLES	I don't know.
MR P.	Well then, one way or another he'll have to leave!
CHARLES	Yes. He has to go.
MR P.	(*With a worried air.*) He has to go. He's the most disconcerting enemy we've ever had. We can't cope with

ahora. No podemos con él, no... Es refractario a todo. (*Impulsivo.*) Carlos, piense usted en algún remedio. Confío mucho en su talento.

DOÑA PEPITA   Bueno. Ya lo estudiaremos despacio. Creo que deberían irse a descansar: es muy tarde.

DON PABLO   Será lo mejor. Pero esta noche tampoco dormiré. ¿Vienes, Pepita?

DOÑA PEPITA   Aún no. Voy a terminar estas notas.

DON PABLO   Buenas noches entonces. No olvide nuestro asunto, Carlos.

(CARLOS *no contesta.*)

DOÑA PEPITA   Adiós. Que descanses. (DON PABLO *se va por la izquierda.* DOÑA PEPITA *se levanta y se acerca a* CARLOS. *Afectuosa, como siempre que se dirige a él*) ¿Usted no se acuesta hoy?

CARLOS   (*Sobresaltado.*) ¿Eh?

DOÑA PEPITA   Pero ¿qué le ocurre, hombre?

CARLOS   (*Tratando de sonreír.*) Nada.

DOÑA PEPITA   Váyase a la cama. Le hace falta.

CARLOS   Sí. Me duele la cabeza. Pero no tengo sueño.

DOÑA PEPITA   Como quiera, hijo. (*Enciende el portátil. Después va al chaflán y apaga la luz central. Vuelve a sentarse y empieza a murmurar repasando sus notas. Escribe. De pronto para la pluma y mira a* CARLOS, *que se está levantando.*) ¿Le dijo a Ignacio que se marchara cuando los vi antes aquí? (CARLOS *no contesta. Su expresión es extrañamente rígida. Lentamente, avanza hacia el chaflán.* DOÑA PEPITA, *sorprendida:*) ¿Se va usted?

CARLOS   (*Reportándose.*) Voy a tomar un poco el aire para despejarme. Que usted descanse. Buenas noches.

(*Sale por el chaflán.*)

DOÑA PEPITA   Buenas noches. Yo me voy ahora también. (*Le ve salir, con gesto conmiserativo. Después prosigue su trabajo. A poco se despereza. Mira el reloj de pulsera.*) Las doce. (*Se levanta y enciende la radio. Manipula. Comienza*

	him, no… he's opposed to everything. (*Impulsively.*) Charles, think of some solution. I've a lot of faith in your ability.[49]
MRS P.	Ok, we'll consider the matter carefully. I think that you should get some rest: it's very late.
MR P.	That'll be the best thing. But tonight'll be another night without sleep. Are you coming, Fran?
MRS P.	Not just yet. I'll finish these notes.
MR P.	Good night, then. Don't forget this business, Charles. (CHARLES *does not reply*.)
MRS P.	Goodbye. Rest now. (MR P. *exits Right*. MRS P. *gets up and goes over to* CHARLES. *As always, when addressing him, she is tender.*) Are you not going to bed tonight?
CHARLES	(*Startled.*) Eh?
MRS P.	But, what's wrong with you, man?
CHARLES	(*Trying to smile.*) Nothing.
MRS P.	Go to bed. You need it.
CHARLES	Yes. I've a sore head. But I'm not tired.
MRS P.	As you wish, my dear. (*She switches on the portable lamp. Then she goes to the curtained doorway and turns off the main light. She sits down again and starts muttering as she checks over her notes. She writes. Suddenly she stops writing and looks at* CHARLES *who is getting up.*) Did you tell Iggy to leave when I saw the pair of you here earlier? (CHARLES *does not reply. His expression is strangely inflexible. Slowly he moves towards the curtained doorway.* MRS P., *in a surprised tone:*) Are you off?
CHARLES	(*Pulling himself together.*) I'm going to get some air to clear my head. You get some rest. Good night. (*He exits by the curtained doorway.*)
MRS P.	Good night. I'm off now as well. (*Full of sympathy, she watches him exit. Then she continues with her work. She stretches. She checks her watch.*) Twelve o'clock. (*She gets up and turns on the radio. She tunes it. A snatch of*

a oírse suavemente un fragmento de «La muerte de
Ase» del Peer Gynt, de Grieg. DOÑA PEPITA *escucha*
unos momentos. Dirige una mirada de desgana a las
cuartillas. Lentamente llega al ventanal y contempla
la noche, con la frente en los cristales. De repente se
estremece. Algo que ve la intriga.) ¿Eh? (*Sigue mirando,*
haciéndose pantalla con las manos. Con tono de
extraordinaria sorpresa:) ¿Qué hacen?

(*Crispa las manos sobre el alféizar. Súbitamente retrocede como si le*
hubiesen dado un golpe en el pecho, mientras lanza un grito ahogado.
Con la faz contraída por el horror, se vuelve. Se lleva las manos a la
boca. Jadea. Al fin corre rápida al chaflán y sale. Por unos momentos
se oye la melodía en la escena sola. Después, gritos lejanos, llamadas.
Pausa. Por la puerta de la izquierda entran rápidamente MIGUELÍN *y*
ANDRÉS.)

ANDRÉS	¿Qué pasa?
MIGUEL	(*Sin dejar de andar.*) No sé. Del campo piden socorro y dicen que vayamos tres o cuatro. Avisa en el dormitorio de la derecha.

(*Salen por el chaflán. Pausa.* ESPERANZA *aparece por la izquierda,*
temblorosa, tanteando el aire. Poco después entra por el chaflán LOLITA,
también muy afectada. Ambas, en bata y pijama.)

ESPERANZA	¿Quién..., quién es?
LOLITA	(*Acercándose.*) ¡Esperanza!

(*Se abrazan, en un rapto de miedo.*)

ESPERANZA	¿Has oído?
LOLITA	Sí.
ESPERANZA	¿Qué ocurre?
LOLITA	¡No lo sé...!

(*Se separa para escuchar.*)

ESPERANZA	¡No me dejes! Tengo miedo.
LOLITA	(*Abrazándose a ella de nuevo.*) *No* se oye nada... Es horrible.

'Aase's Death' from Peer Gynt by Grieg is heard softly playing. MRS P. *listens for a few moments. She looks half-heartedly at the sheets of paper. She slowly goes over to the large window and looks out at the night, with her face pressed to the pane. Suddenly she shudders. She is intrigued by something she sees.*) Eh? (*She continues looking, with her hands raised in the form of a visor. In a remarkably surprised tone:*) What are they doing? (*She grips the windowsill. Suddenly she steps back as though she had been struck in the chest, and lets out a muffled cry. With her face contorted in horror, she turns round. She puts her hands to her mouth. She gasps. Finally she runs quickly to the curtained doorway and exits. For a few moments the melody is all that is heard on stage. Then, distant shouting and calls. A pause. Through the door on the Right* MIKEY *and* ANDY *enter quickly.*)[50]

ANDY   What's happening?

MIKEY   (*Without breaking stride.*) I don't know. They're shouting for help from the field, they want three or four of us. Tell them in the dorm on the right. (*They exit by the curtained doorway. A pause.* HOPE *appears to the Right, trembling and groping in the air. Shortly afterwards* LINDA *enters by the curtained doorway, she is also very affected by it all. Both are wearing dressing gowns and pyjamas.*)

HOPE   Who... who's there?

LINDA   (*Approaching.*) Hope! (*They embrace in fear.*)

HOPE   Did you hear?

LINDA   Yes.

HOPE   What's going on?

LINDA   I don't know... (*She moves away to listen.*)

HOPE   Don't leave me. I'm afraid.

LINDA   (*Clinging on to her again.*) You can't hear anything... it's dreadful.

ESPERANZA	(*Cayendo de rodillas.*) ¡Dios mío, piedad!
LOLITA	¡No me asustes! ¡Levanta!

(*La ayuda a hacerlo.*)

ESPERANZA	Tengo la sensación de algo irreparable...
LOLITA	¡Calla!
ESPERANZA	Como si hubiésemos estado cometiendo un gran error. Me siento vacía... Y sola...
LOLITA	¡Oigo pasos! (*Se enfrenta con el chaflán.*) ¡Vámonos!
ESPERANZA	(*Reteniéndola por una mano.*) ¡No me dejes, Lolita! Estoy llena de pena... Duerme esta noche conmigo.
LOLITA	¡Se acercan!
ESPERANZA	¡Ven a mi alcoba! Es terrible esta soledad.
LOLITA	Vamos, sí... Tengo frío...

(*Se apresuran a salir por la izquierda, muy inquietas. Pausa. Se oyen murmullos después y entran por el chaflán* DOÑA PEPITA, *que enciende en seguida la luz central, y tras ella* ALBERTO *y* ANDRÉS, *que traen el cadáver de* IGNACIO, *cuya cabeza cuelga y se bambolea. Tras ellos,* MIGUELÍN, PEDRO *y* CARLOS. *Vienen agitados, pálidos de emoción.*)

DOÑA PEPITA	Colóquenlo aquí, en el sofá. ¡Aprisa! Miguelín, apague esa radio, por favor. (MIGUELÍN *lo hace y queda junto al aparato.* DOÑA PEPITA *toca el brazo de* ANDRÉS.) Andrés, avise en seguida a don Pablo, se lo ruego.
ANDRÉS	Ahora mismo.

(*Se va por la izquierda.*)

DOÑA PEPITA	(*Arrodillada, coge la muñeca de* IGNACIO *y le pone el oído junto al corazón.*) ¡Está muerto!

(*Con los ojos desorbitados, mira a* CARLOS, *que permanece impasible. Entra precipitadamente por la izquierda* DON PABLO. *Viene a medio vestir y sin gafas. Detrás de él entra de nuevo* ANDRÉS.)

DON PABLO	¿Qué pasa? ¿Qué le ha ocurrido a Ignacio? ¿Estás aquí, Pepita?
DOÑA PEPITA	Ignacio se ha matado. Está aquí, sobre el sofá.
DON PABLO	¿Se ha matado?... ¡No comprendo! (*Avanza hacia el sofá. Se inclina. Palpa.*) ¿Cómo ha ocurrido? ¿Dónde?

HOPE	(*Falling to her knees.*) God have mercy on us!
LINDA	Don't scare me! Get up! (*She helps her to do so.*)
HOPE	I sense something seriously bad…
LINDA	Quiet!
HOPE	As though we've been making a huge mistake. I feel empty… and alone…
LINDA	I hear footsteps. (*She comes up against the curtained doorway.*) Let's get out of here!
HOPE	(*Holding her back by the hand.*) Don't leave me, Linda. I feel awful…sleep in my bed tonight.
LINDA	They're coming!
HOPE	Come to my room. It's terrible being alone.
LINDA	Yes, let's go… I'm cold… (*Very anxious, they hurry off Right. A pause. Then murmurs are heard and by the curtained doorway enters* MRS P., *who immediately turns on the main light, followed by* AL *and* ANDY *who are carrying the body of* IGGY, *whose head is hanging and swaying. Behind them are* MIKEY, PETE *and* CHARLES. *Pale with emotion, they are in a state of anxiety.*)
MRS P.	Put him here, on the sofa. Hurry! Mikey, turn that radio off, please. (MIKEY *does so and stays beside the music system.* MRS P. *taps* ANDY *on the arm.*) Andy, tell Mr P. at once, I beg you.
ANDY	At once. (*He exits Right.*)
MRS P.	(*Kneeling, takes* IGGY's *wrist and puts her ear close to his chest.*) He's dead! (*With her eyes standing out of her head, she looks at* CHARLES, *who remains impassive.* MR P. *enters quickly from the Right. He's half-dressed and is not wearing his glasses. Behind him* ANDY *re-enters.*)
MR P.	What's up? What's happened to Iggy? Are you there, Fran?
MRS P.	Iggy's been killed. He's here on the sofa.
MR P.	He's been killed?… I don't understand! (*He moves to the sofa. He bends down. He feels around.*) How did it happen? Where did it happen?

DOÑA PEPITA   En el campo de deportes. Yo realmente no sé... Llegué después.

DON PABLO   ¿No sabe nadie cómo ha sido? ¿Quién lo encontró primero?

CARLOS   Yo.

(DOÑA PEPITA *no le pierde de vista.*)

DON PABLO   ¡Ah! Cuéntenos, cuéntenos, Carlos.

CARLOS   Poco puedo decir. Había salido para tomar el aire porque me dolía la cabeza. Me pareció oír ruidos hacia el tobogán... Me fui acercando. Al tiempo de llegar sentí un golpe sordo, muy fuerte. Y el movimiento del aire. Comprendí en seguida que debía tratarse de alguna desgracia. Llegué y palpé. Me pareció que era Ignacio. Se había caído desde la torreta y a su lado había una de las esterillas que se usan para el descenso. Entonces pedí socorro. Doña Pepita llegó en seguida y gritamos más... Después lo hemos traído aquí.

(*Entretanto,* DOÑA PEPITA *ha cubierto al muerto con el tapete de una de las mesitas.*)

DON PABLO   ¿Cómo es posible? ¡Ahora lo entiendo menos! No comprendo qué tenía que hacer Ignacio subido a estas horas en la torreta del tobogán...

ANDRÉS   Acaso se trate de un suicidio, don Pablo.

ALBERTO   ¿Y para qué quería la esterilla, entonces? Ignacio se ha matado cuando intentaba deslizarse por el tobogán. Eso está muy claro. Ya sabemos que era muy torpe para todo.

DON PABLO   Pero él no era hombre para esas cosas... ¿Qué le importaba el juego del tobogán? Por su misma torpeza no quiso nunca entrenarse con ustedes en ningún deporte.

MIGUEL   Permita, don Pablo, que el alumno más joven dé quizá con la razón que ustedes no encuentran. (*Expectación.*) Yo conocía muy bien a Ignacio. (*Dolorosamente.*) Precisamente porque le torturaban tanto sus miserias, acaso tratase de superarlas en secreto, simulando indiferencia por los juegos frente a nosotros. Creo que

MRS P.	On the sports field. I really don't know... I arrived afterwards.
MR P.	Does anyone know what's happened? Who found him first?
CHARLES	I did. (MRS P. *keeps a sharp eye on him.*)
MR P.	Right! Tell us, tell us, Charles.
CHARLES	I can't tell much. I'd gone out to get some air because I'd a headache. I thought I heard noises over towards the toboggan run... I went over. Just as I got there I heard a really heavy dull thud. And movement in the air. I realised at once that something terrible must have happened. I reached the spot and felt my way. It seemed to be Iggy. He had fallen from the tower and beside him was one of the mats you use to slide down. Then I called for help. Mrs P. arrived at once and we called out again... Then we brought him here. (*Meanwhile,* MRS P. *has covered the body with a cloth from one of the tables.*)
MR P.	How can this be? I just don't understand. I don't understand what possessed Iggy to go up the tower of the toboggan run at this hour of the night...
ANDY	Maybe we're talking suicide, Mr P.
AL	So what was he doing with the mat, then? Iggy's got himself killed trying to slide down the toboggan run. That's very clear. We know how really clumsy he was.
MR P.	But he wasn't one for those things... What did he care about tobogganing? Because of his clumsiness he never wanted to train with you people for any sport.
MIKEY	Mr P., allow the youngest student to maybe come up with the explanation none of you can find. (*There is a sense of expectancy.*) I knew Iggy very well. (*Painfully.*) For the very reason that his misfortunes tortured him so, he perhaps tried to overcome them in private, letting on to us he didn't care about activities. I think that tonight and

esta noche y muchas otras, seguramente, en que tardaba en llegar a nuestro cuarto, trataba de adquirir destreza sin necesidad de pasar por el ridículo. Ya saben que era muy susceptible...

DON PABLO   (*«A moro muerto, gran lanzada».*) En vez de aprender cuando se le indicaba, nos busca ahora esta complicación por su mala cabeza. Espero que esto sirva de lección a todos... (*Breve pausa, durante la que los estudiantes desvían la cabeza, avergonzados.*) Sí. Seguramente eso es lo que pasó. ¿No te parece, Pepita?

DOÑA PEPITA   (*Sin dejar de mirar a* CARLOS.) Es muy posible.

DON PABLO   ¿Qué opina usted, Carlos?

CARLOS   Me parece que Miguelín ha dado en el clavo.

DON PABLO   Menos mal. La hipótesis del suicidio era muy desagradable. No hubiera compaginado bien con la moral de nuestro centro.

DOÑA PEPITA   ¿Quieres que vaya a telefonear?

DON PABLO   Es más indicado que vaya yo. Al padre también tendré que avisarle... ¡Pobre hombre! Recuerdo que me habló con miedo de los accidentes... ¡Pero un accidente puede ocurrirle a cualquiera, y nosotros podemos demostrar que el tobogán y los otros juegos responden a una adecuada pedagogía! ¿Verdad, Pepita?

DOÑA PEPITA   Sí, anda. No te preocupes por eso. Yo me quedaré aquí.

DON PABLO   El muy... ¡torpe! trataba de... ¡Claro!

(*Se va por el chaflán. Entra por la izquierda, aún vestida,* ELISA. *Se detiene cerca de la puerta.*)

ELISA   ¿Qué ha pasado? Dicen por ahí que Ignacio...

MIGUEL   Ignacio se ha matado. Aquí está su cadáver.

ELISA   (*Con sorpresa y sin emoción.*) ¡Oh!

(*Instintivamente se acerca a* MIGUELÍN *hasta tocarlo. Desliza sus manos por la cintura de él, en un expresivo gesto de reapropiación.* MIGUELÍN *le rodea fuertemente el talle. Poco a poco,* ELISA *reclina la cabeza sobre el hombro de* MIGUELÍN.)

	on many other nights, no doubt, when he was slow about coming back to our room, he was trying to practise the skills he needed without making a fool of himself in public. You know he was very touchy about…
MR P.	(*Acting tough.*) Instead of learning when training was being provided, he messes things up for us all because his head's not straight. I hope that's a lesson for everyone… (*A brief pause, during which the students turn away in shame.*) Yes. That's surely what happened! What do you think, Fran?
MRS P.	(*Without taking her eyes off* CHARLES.) It's very likely.
MR P.	What do you think, Charles?
CHARLES	I think Mikey's hit the nail on the head.
MR P.	Just as well. The suicide theory was very unpleasant. It wouldn't have helped the morale of our Centre.[51]
MRS P.	Do you want me to go and phone?
MR P.	Better I do it. I'll have to tell the father… Poor chap! I remember he spoke to me in fear about accidents… But an accident can happen to anyone, and we can show that the toboggan run and the other activities correspond to a suitable curriculum! Right, Fran?
MRS P.	Yes, fine. Don't worry about that. I'll stay here.
MR P.	The clumsy…boy tried to… That's it! (*He exits by the curtained doorway. Enter* LISA, *still dressed, from the Right. She stops near the door.*)
LISA	What's happened? They're saying that Iggy…
MIKEY	Iggy's dead. Here's his corpse.
LISA	(*Surprised, but unemotional.*) Oh! (*Instinctively she approaches* MIKEY *until she makes contact with him. She runs her hands over his waist in a meaningful reclaiming gesture.* MIKEY *puts his arm firmly round her waist. Gradually,* LISA *lowers her head onto* MIKEY's *shoulder.*)

DOÑA PEPITA	Creo que deben marcharse todos de aquí. Muchas gracias por su ayuda y procuren no comentar demasiado con los compañeros. Buenas noches. (*Despide con palmaditas en el hombro a* PEDRO *y a* ALBERTO *por el chaflán.*) Recomienden que no venga nadie a esta habitación.

(ANDRÉS *se va también por la izquierda. Tras él,* MIGUELÍN *y* ELISA, *enlazados. Él va serio y tranquilo. Ella no puede evitar una sonrisa feliz.*)

ELISA	Casi es mejor para él... No estaba hecho para la vida. ¿No te parece, Miguelín?
MIGUEL	(*Cariñoso.*) Sí. Ha sido lo mejor que le podía ocurrir. Es muy torpe para todo.

(*Se oyen por la izquierda las llamadas de* JUANA, *que aparece en seguida, con bata, cruzando ante ellos.* MIGUELÍN, *contristado, intenta detenerla, mas* ELISA *lo retiene de nuevo, suave, y lo conduce a la puerta, por donde salen.*)

JUANA	¡Carlos! ¡Carlos! ¿Estás aquí?
CARLOS	Aquí estoy, Juana.

(*Ella le encuentra en el primer término y se arroja en sus brazos sollozando.*)

JUANA	¡Carlos! (CARLOS *la acoge con una desencantada sonrisa.* DOÑA PEPITA *los mira dolorosamente.*) ¡Pobre Ignacio!
CARLOS	Ya descansa.
JUANA	Sí. Ahora es más feliz. (*Llora.*) ¡Perdóname! Sé que te he hecho sufrir...
CARLOS	No tengo nada que perdonarte, querida mía.
JUANA	¡Sí, sí! Tengo que confesarte muchas cosas... Me pesan horriblemente... Pero mi intención era buena, ¡te lo juro! ¡Yo nunca he dejado de quererte, Carlos!
CARLOS	Lo sé, Juana, lo sé.
JUANA	¿Me perdonarás? ¡Te lo confesaré todo! ¡Todo!
CARLOS	No es preciso, ya que nada grave puede ser. Te lo perdono todo sin saberlo.

MRS P. I think everyone should leave here. Many thanks for your help and try not to say too much about this to the others. Good night. (*She ushers* PETE *and* AL *out of the curtained doorway with gentle pats on the back.*) Tell them nobody's to come to this room. (ANDY *too exits Right. Behind him go* MIKEY *and* LISA *arm-in-arm. He is serious and calm. She cannot help giving a happy smile.*)

LISA It's almost better for him... He wasn't made for this life. Eh, Mikey?

MIKEY (*Tenderly.*)Yeah, it's the best thing that could have happened to him. He was very clumsy at everything. (*To the Right are heard calls from* JANE *who appears at once, in her dressing gown, crossing in front of the others.* MIKEY, *saddened, tries to stop her, but* LISA *takes hold of him again, gently, and leads him to the door, through which they exit.*)

JANE Charles! Charles! Are you there?

CHARLES I'm here, Jane. (*She finds him Down-stage and throws herself weeping into his arms.*)

JANE Charles! (CHARLES *receives her with a disillusioned smile.* MRS P. *watches them sorrowfully.*) Poor Iggy!

CHARLES He's at peace now.

JANE Yes, now he's happier. (*She cries.*) Forgive me! I know I've made you suffer...

CHARLES There's nothing for me to forgive you for, my darling.

JANE Yes, there is! I have to confess lots to you... It's weighing me down awfully... But my intentions were good, I swear! I never stopped loving you, Charles!

CHARLES I know, Jane, I know.

JANE Will you forgive me? I'll tell you everything! Everything!

CHARLES That's not necessary, it can't be anything serious. I forgive you it all without knowing what it was.

JUANA | ¡Carlos! (*Le besa impulsivamente.*)
DOÑA PEPITA | (*Sombría.*) Será mejor que vuelva a su cuarto, señorita.
CARLOS | Tiene usted razón. Vamos, Juanita. Debemos marcharnos.

(*Enlazados; él, melancólico, y ella, vibrando, se dirigen a la izquierda.*)

DOÑA PEPITA | (*Con trabajo.*) Usted quédese, Carlos. Quiero hablarle.
CARLOS | (*Inclina la cabeza.*) Está bien. Adiós, Juana.
JUANA | Hasta mañana, Carlos. ¡Y gracias!

(*Separan lentamente sus manos.* JUANA *se va.* CARLOS *queda en pie, aguardando.* DOÑA PEPITA *lo mira angustiada. Una larga pausa.*)

DOÑA PEPITA | Ha sido lamentable, ¿verdad?
CARLOS | Sí.

(*Pausa.*)

DOÑA PEPITA | (*Se acerca, mirándole fijamente.*) Sería inútil negar que el centro se ha librado de su mayor pesadilla... Que todos vamos a descansar y a revivir... La solución que antes reclamaba don Pablo... se ha dado ya. (*Con acento de reproche.*) ¡Pero nadie esperaba... tanto!
CARLOS | (*Terminante.*) Sea como sea, el peligro se cortó a tiempo.
DOÑA PEPITA | (*Amarga.*) ¿Usted cree?
CARLOS | (*Despectivo.*) ¿No se dio cuenta? Muerto Ignacio, sus mejores amigos le abandonan; murmuran sobre su cadáver. ¡Ah, los ciegos, los ciegos! ¡Se creen con derecho a compadecerle; ellos, que son pequeños y vulgares! Miguelín y Elisa se reconcilian. Los demás respiran como si les hubiesen librado de un gran peso. ¡Vuelve la alegría a la casa! ¡Todo se arregla!
DOÑA PEPITA | Me apena oírle...
CARLOS | (*Violento.*) ¿Por qué?

(*Breve pausa.*)

DOÑA PEPITA | (*En un arranque.*) ¡Qué ha hecho usted!

JANE	Charles! (*She kisses him impulsively.*)
MRS P.	(*Gloomily.*) It'd be better if you returned to your room, young lady.
CHARLES	You're right. Let's go, Janey. We must leave. (*Arm-in-arm they head Left, he downcast and she trembling.*)
MRS P.	(*Strongly.*) Stay, Charles. I want to talk to you.
CHARLES	(*Lowers his head.*) Ok. Bye, Jane.
JANE	See you tomorrow, Charles. And thanks![52] (*They let go of each other's hands slowly.* JANE *exits.* CHARLES *remains standing, waiting.* MRS P. *gives him an anguished look. A long pause.*)
MRS P.	Dreadful, wasn't it?
CHARLES	Yes. (*A pause.*)
MRS P.	(*She approaches, fixing her gaze on him.*) It'd be pointless to deny that the Centre's been relieved of its biggest nightmare... that we're all going to rest up and turn things round... The solution Mr P. wanted earlier... has now been delivered. (*In a reproachful tone.*) But nobody expected... all this!
CHARLES	(*Categorically.*) Whatever, the danger's been nipped in the bud.
MRS P.	(*Bitterly.*) Do you think so?
CHARLES	(*Contemptuously.*) Don't you realise? With Iggy dead, his best friends have given up on him; they're muttering platitudes over his corpse. Ah, the blind, that's the blind for you! They think they've the right to feel sorry for him, but they're small and insignificant! Mikey and Lisa get back together. The others breathe easily as though a great weight's been lifted off them. The place is happy again! Everything's ok now!
MRS P.	It pains me to hear you...
CHARLES	(*Vehemently.*) Why? (*A brief pause.*)
MRS P.	(*Blurting it out.*) Because of what you've done!

CARLOS	(*Irguiéndose.*) No comprendo qué quiere decir.
DOÑA PEPITA	A veces, Carlos, creemos hacer un bien y cometemos un grave error...
CARLOS	No sé a qué se refiere.
DOÑA PEPITA	Tampoco acertamos a comprender, a veces, que no se nos habla para inquietarnos, sino para consolarnos... Se nos acercan personas que nos quieren y sufren al vernos sufrir, y no queremos entenderlo... Las rechazamos cuando más desesperadamente necesitamos descansar en un pecho amigo...
CARLOS	(*Frío.*) Muchas gracias por su afecto..., que es innecesario ahora.
DOÑA PEPITA	(*Cogiéndole las manos.*) ¡Hijo!
CARLOS	(*Desasiéndose.*) No soy tonto, doña Pepita. Comprendo de sobra lo que insinúa. Ignacio y yo, a la misma hora, en el campo de deportes... Esa suposición es falsa.
DOÑA PEPITA	¡Claro que sí! ¡Falsa! No he dicho yo otra cosa. (*Lenta.*) Ni pienso decir otra cosa.
CARLOS	No puedo agradecérselo. Nada hice.
DOÑA PEPITA	(*Con una fugaz mirada al muerto.*) Y el pobre Ignacio ya nada podrá decir. Pero cálmese, Carlos... Suponiendo que fuese cierto... (*Movimiento de él.*) ¡Ya, ya sé que no lo es! Pero en el caso de que lo fuese, nada podría arreglarse ya hablando..., y el centro está por encima de todo.
CARLOS	Opino lo mismo.
DOÑA PEPITA	Y todos nuestros actos deben tender a beneficiarle, ¿no es así?
CARLOS	(*Irónico.*) Así es. Sé lo que piensa; no se canse.
DOÑA PEPITA	O a beneficiarnos personalmente.
CARLOS	¿Qué?
DOÑA PEPITA	El centro puede tener enemigos..., y las personas, rivales de amor. (*Pausa. CARLOS se vuelve y avanza cansadamente hacia la derecha. Tropieza en una silla del juego de ajedrez y se deja caer en ella.*) ¿No quiere confiarse a mí?

CHARLES	(*Prickly*) I don't understand what you mean.
MRS P.	Sometimes, Charles, we think we're doing good and we make a serious mistake…
CHARLES	I don't know what you're getting at.
MRS P.	And neither do we manage to understand, sometimes, that people don't talk to us to worry us, but rather to console us… People come to us who love us and they suffer because they see us suffering, and we don't want to understand… We reject them at the very time when we most desperately need a friendly shoulder to cry on…
CHARLES	(*Coldly.*) Thanks a lot for your affection… which isn't needed now.
MRS P.	(*Taking him by the hands.*) Son!
CHARLES	(*Freeing himself.*) I'm not stupid, Mrs P. I understand only too well what you're hinting at. Iggy and myself at the same time on the sports field… That theory is false.
MRS P.	Of course it is! It's false! I didn't say otherwise. (*Slowly.*) Nor do I intend to.
CHARLES	I can't thank you for that. I did nothing.
MRS P.	(*With a fleeting glance at the corpse.*) And poor Iggy won't be able to say anything… But, calm down, Charles… Even if it were true… (*He moves around.*) And, yes, I know it isn't! But if it were, nothing would be sorted out by talking to…, and the Centre comes before everything else.
CHARLES	I agree.
MRS P.	And everything we do must be for its benefit, isn't that right?
CHARLES	(*Ironically.*) That's it. I know what you're thinking: don't labour it.
MRS P.	Or for our personal benefit.
CHARLES	What?
MRS P.	The Centre may well have enemies…, and people have rivals in love. (*A pause.* CHARLES *turns round and moves wearily to the Left. He bumps into a chair by the chessboard and flops down into it.*) Don't you want to confide in me?

CARLOS   (*Tenaz.*) ¡Le repito que es falso lo que piensa!
DOÑA PEPITA   (*Que se acerca por detrás y apoya sus manos en los hombros de él.*) Bien... Me he engañado. No ha habido ningún crimen; ni siquiera un crimen pasional. Usted no quiere provocar la piedad de nadie. ¿Ni de Juana?
CARLOS   (*Feroz.*) Juana deberá aprender a evitar ese peligroso sentimiento.

(*Pausa. Su mano juguetea con las piezas del tablero.*)

DOÑA PEPITA   Carlos...
CARLOS   Qué.
DOÑA PEPITA   Le haría tanto bien abandonarse...
CARLOS   (*Levantándose de golpe.*) ¡Basta! ¡No se obstine en conseguir una confesión imposible! ¿Qué pretende? ¿Acreditar su sagacidad? ¿Representar conmigo el papel de madre a falta de hijos propios?
DOÑA PEPITA   (*Lívida.*) Es usted cruel... No lo seré yo tanto. Porque hace media hora yo trabajaba aquí, y pudo ocurrírseme levantarme para mirar por el ventanal. No lo hice. Acaso, de hacerlo, habría visto a alguien que subía las escaleras del tobogán cargado con el cuerpo de Ignacio... ¡Ignacio desvanecido, o quizá ya muerto! (*Pausa.*) Luego, desde arriba, se precipita el cuerpo..., sin tener la precaución de pensar en los ojos de los demás. Siempre olvidamos la vista ajena. Sólo Ignacio pensaba en ella. (*Pausa.*) Pero yo no vi nada, porque no me levanté.

(*Aguarda, espiando su rostro.*)

CARLOS   ¡No, no vio nada! Y aunque se hubiese levantado y hubiese creído ver... (*Con infinito desprecio.*) ¿Qué es la vista? ¡No existe aquí la vista! ¿Cómo se atreve a invocar el testimonio de sus ojos? ¡Sus ojos! ¡Bah!
DOÑA PEPITA   (*Llorosa.*) Hijo mío, no es bueno ser tan duro.
CARLOS   ¡Déjeme! ¡Y no intente vencerme con sus repugnantes argucias femeninas!
DOÑA PEPITA   Olvida que soy casi una vieja...
CARLOS   ¡Usted es quien parece haberlo olvidado!

CHARLES	(*Tenaciously.*) I tell you again, what you're thinking is wrong!
MRS P.	(*Who approaches from behind and rests her hands on his shoulders.*) Ok... I've got it wrong. There was no crime; not even a crime of passion. You don't want pity from anyone. Not even from Jane?
CHARLES	(*Fiercely.*) Jane will have to learn to side-step that dangerous emotion. (*A pause. He plays with the chess pieces in his hand.*)
MRS P.	Charles.
CHARLES	Yeah.
MRS P.	It'd be so good for you to let it all out...
CHARLES	(*Rising suddenly.*) That's enough! Don't harp on after an impossible confession! What are you trying to do? Prove your wisdom? Playing the role of mother with me, because you don't have children of your own?
MRS P.	(*Furiously.*) You're cruel... I won't be so cruel. Because half an hour ago I was working here, and it could have occurred to me to get up and look through the large window. I didn't. Perhaps if I had done, I'd have seen someone going up the steps of the toboggan run loaded down with Iggy's body... Iggy out cold, or perhaps already dead! (*A pause.*) Then, from above, the body's thrown down..., without taking the precaution of thinking of other people's eyes. We always forget what others can see. Only Iggy thought of that. (*A pause.*) But I saw nothing, because I didn't get up. (*She waits, studying his face.*)[53]
CHARLES	You saw nothing! And even if you had got up and had thought you saw... (*With real disdain.*) What is sight? Sight doesn't exist here! How can you dare to call your eyes as witnesses? Your eyes! Bah![54]
MRS P.	(*Tearfully.*) Son, it's not good to be so hard.
CHARLES	Leave me be! And don't try to defeat me with your repulsive feminine wiles!
MRS P.	You're forgetting that I'm almost an old woman...
CHARLES	You're the one who seems to have forgotten that!

DOÑA PEPITA ¿Qué dice? (*Llorando.*) ¡Loco, está usted loco!...

CARLOS (*Desesperado.*) ¡Sí! ¡Márchese!

(*Pausa.*)

DOÑA PEPITA (*Turbada.*) Sí, me voy... Parece que don Pablo tarda demasiado... (*Inicia la marcha y se detiene.*) Y usted no quiere amistad, ni paz... No quiere paz ahora. Porque cree haber vencido, y eso le basta. Pero usted no ha vencido, Carlos; acuérdese de lo que le digo... Usted no ha vencido.

(*Engloba en una triste mirada al asesino y a su víctima, y sale por el chaflán.* CARLOS *se derrumba sobre la silla. Su cabeza pierde la rigidez anterior y se dobla sobre el pecho. Su respiración es a cada momento más agitada: al fin no puede más y se despechuga, despojándose, con un gesto que es mitad de ahogo y mitad de indiferencia, de la corbata. Después vuelve la cabeza hacia el fondo, como si atendiese a alguna inaudible llamada. Luego se levanta, vacilante. Al hacerlo, derriba involuntariamente con la manga las fichas del tablero, que ponen con su discordante ruido una nota agria y brutal en el momento. Se detiene un segundo, asustado por el percance, y palpa con tristeza las fichas. Después avanza haca el cadáver. Ya a su lado, en la suprema amargura de su soledad irremediable, cae de rodillas y descubre con un gesto brusco la pálida faz del muerto, que toca con la desesperanza de quien toca a un dormido que ya no podrá despertar. Luego se levanta, como atraído por una fuerza extraña, y se acerca tanteando al ventanal. Allí queda inmóvil, frente a la luz de las estrellas. Una voz grave, que pronto se encandece y vibra de pasión infinita – la suya –, comienza a oírse.*)

CARLOS ... Y ahora están brillando las estrellas con todo su esplendor, y los videntes gozan de su presencia maravillosa. Esos mundos lejanísimos están ahí, tras los cristales... (*Sus manos, como las alas de un pájaro herido, tiemblan y repiquetean contra la cárcel misteriosa del cristal.*) ¡Al alcance de nuestra vista!..., si la tuviéramos...

TELÓN LENTO

MRS P.   What are you saying? (*Crying.*) You're mad, mad!...

CHARLES   (*Despairingly.*) Yeah, get out of here! (*A pause.*)

MRS P.   (*Upset.*) Yes, I'm going... It seems Mr P.'s taking too long... (*She starts walking and stops.*) And you want neither friendship nor peace... you don't want peace now. Because you think you've won and that's enough for you... But you haven't won, Charles; mark my words... You haven't won.

(*With a sad gaze she takes in the murderer and his victim,*[55] *and exits by the curtained doorway.* CHARLES *collapses into the seat. His head loses its earlier rigidity and slumps to his chest. His breathing grows increasingly more agitated: finally he can bear it no longer and he loosens his collar, taking off his tie with a gesture that is half breathlessness, half indifference. Then he turns his head back, as though listening to some inaudible call. Next, he gets up, hesitantly. On doing so, he accidentally knocks over the chess pieces with his sleeve; that discordant noise introduces a bitter, brutal note in the proceedings. He stops for a moment, stunned by the mishap, and sadly gropes the pieces. Then he moves towards the corpse. Once beside it, in the utter bitterness of his irreparable solitude, he falls to his knees and brusquely uncovers the pale face of the deceased, which he touches with the despair of someone touching a sleeping figure whom he will not be able to waken. Then he gets up, as though pulled by a strange force, and gropes his way towards the large window. There he remains motionless, facing the light of the stars. A solemn voice, which soon crackles and vibrates with boundless passion – his own – begins to be heard.*)

CHARLES   ...And right now the stars are shining in all their splendour, and seers are enjoying the wonder of their presence. Those very distant worlds are there, beyond this glass... (*His hands, like the wings of a wounded bird, tremble and knock against the mysterious cell that is the glass.*) Within range of our sight!..., if we had sight...[56]

SLOW CURTAIN

Buero-Vallejo with the King and Queen of Spain, Juan Carlos and Sofía, in 1997
at the premiere of the revival of his 1967 play 'El Tragaluz' ('The Skylight').

NOTES

1. Miguel Hernández (1910–1942), a celebrated poet in his own right, met Buero-Vallejo in the hospital in Benicasim during the Spanish Civil War. The subject of a fine portrait by Buero drawn in the jail in Conde De Toreno, he died in prison in Alicante.
2. Note the playwright's typically detailed – almost fussy – stage directions. Note also that the directions Right and Left are seen differently in the Spanish-speaking and English-speaking theatre worlds: the former sees the action from the spectators' perspective, the latter, from the actors'.

   The "ample foliage" here is significant: at this point the Centre and its values are in full bloom, but will subsequently wither when Iggy exerts his influence. "The illusion of normality" is also a key phrase and is what the Centre seeks to promote. Charles and Jane are very much the ideal couple, at the top of the student hierarchy: note how well and conventionally turned out he is and how she is described as – rather stereotypically – "pretty and sweet".
3. Mikey's jocular, lively presence ignites the others. We note, however, that Charles and Jane do not respond instantly to him by immediately going to shake his hand as the others do. Even in the start-of-term euphoria they are slightly aloof and more measured.
4. The stick (or cane), which Mikey evidently uses in the outside world (that is, out-of-term), is banned in-term in the Centre, where students are supposed to be confident and self-reliant with regard to walking around. Of course, the stick-wielding Iggy is soon to appear on stage.
5. Enter the classic mysterious stranger, clad in black. Iggy's (shoddy) appearance contrasts with Charles'.
6. Jane tells a lie: *she* took *his* hand.
7. Note Iggy's initially self-pitying attitude and the boys' subsequent aggressive response to this even very slight and early sign of weakness by a blind person. They are programmed – almost Pavlovianly – not to show such signs and, indeed, to suppress them.
8. Charles hesitates to use the word "blind" ("*ciegos*").
9. The alleged "pedagogical theory" will eventually be seen to amount to a method of hiding the truth.
10. Charles is initially – almost instinctively – decent towards Iggy. Does this show that he is basically a good, upright individual?
11. We notice Buero's insistence here on "activities" ("*juegos*" are literally "games") which the Centre promotes to sustain that "illusion of normality". The Father's question is, of course, a terribly ironic one in the light of events in Act III.
12. The Centre's approved parlance comes to the fore: blind people are "non-seers"; the place has a "morale of steel" – a phrase so resonant that the Father uses it minutes later. Do we detect also a slightly menacing tone in Mr P.'s "friendly advice"?

13. Another item from the approved lexicon: "seer" ("*vidente*"). Note Iggy's reaction.
14. A phrase which, as pointed out elsewhere in this edition, forms part of the linguistic consistency to Iggy's attack on the Establishment.
15. Mr P. is not much of a psychologist.
16. The "happiness zone" is a phrase associated here with Charles; but really it has the ring of another piece of Centre-speak. Interestingly, the girls here only seem to define themselves in terms of the men in their lives.
17. More "linguistic consistency" from Iggy.
18. Jane strikes the wrong chord with Iggy: she talks of "a girlfriend", when he is looking for profound love.
19. Some rather Sartrian/Camusian-sounding lines here from Iggy, who refers to suffering, confrontation and collaboration. Iggy totally rejects Centre-speak. Jane cannot subsequently cope with or counter his impassioned argument and is reduced to begging him to stay. It is perhaps a dramatic (not to say, logical) weakness that he suddenly decides to do so.
20. Iggy's rhetoric about war, peace and fire culminates with what is for him a bottom line: "...I want to see!".
21. Although he quickly regains his verbal poise, Charles' moment of anxiety and indecision is well and significantly captured. His girlfriend has left him to it, and he is, at least momentarily, reduced to the stereoptype of a blind person groping in the darkness.
22. Time has moved on, and the season has changed to what looks like late Autumn. Symbolically, of course, the Centre too (and what it represents) has withered like the leaves on the trees.
23. In English, or in Spanish, there is just a hint of something sinister here.
24. A crucial detail; Iggy has broken the special link that held the group together.
25. Battle is about to be joined – in terms familiar to Iggy.
26. Here, as elsewhere, Iggy is seen as a pestilence, a disease to be eradicated.
27. It is philosophically significant that Reason is recruited to the Establishment's cause. The Cartesians are lining up against the Existentialist.
28. Iggy is about to tell his story, as Christ would have told a parable to his disciples. In this case the lesson is about the harsh reality of blindness.
29. Iggy disdains Mikey's frivolous, quasi-Berkeleian ("*esse est percepi*") syllogism.
30. Iggy is up to something: lifting the ashtray, moving the table, and covering his actions by the Socratic ploy of speaking while on the move. He is about to demonstrate to Charles how the latter's "security is an illusion", and Charles will fail the test when he audibly stumbles and hesitates: one up for Existentialism over Cartesian Rationalism.
31. Iggy goes too far, unaware that Mrs P. is listening.
32. An Oedipal affair?
33. By acting so loudly, Charles lets Iggy know that he realises what Iggy has done.
34. A telling phrase, uttered shortly after we are made aware of another symbolic sign of Iggy's disruptive effect on his fellow students: their recent tendency to fall and stumble around the ice-rink.
35. Iggy hears all of this, including the "Christ crucified" comment, and must now fully realise the effect he is having on the other students.

36. Besides worrying about the loss of her Mikey to Iggy's cause, Lisa is now concerned that even Jane may be lost to Iggy.
37. The dénouement of Act II: Jane (who is effectively only a pawn in the "war" between Charles and the increasingly assured Iggy) asks Iggy to leave but he, in return, declares his love for her, in a basic, pragmatic, but sincere manner.
38. The stage direction here – "(seriously)" – seems to indicate that Charles has surmised who the kissing parties were.
39. Charles' dishevelled appearance mirrors his crestfallen state. However, we then note how different (and steely) his reaction is to his "loss", compared to Lisa's to hers.
40. Charles' mind seems clear. This is sinister-sounding.
41. A rare moment in which Iggy is off-guard.
42. Charles' words here – as he and Iggy have the stage to themselves – are subtly menacing, as he leads in to asking Iggy to leave the Centre.
43. A fine piece of rhetoric from Iggy: the key passage here is, of course, repeated by Charles just before the final curtain.
44. This is what Iggy is all about: his words are so potent that Charles is momentarily affected, and goes on to use the word "blind".
45. Total darkness: designed to elicit empathy from the audience.
46. Ironically, Iggy does not realise how close he is to achieving that "vision".
47. Is Iggy right when he claims that Charles is motivated by the loss of Jane? Whatever the case may be, the play is taking a very marked Existentialist turn here: suicide has been considered as an option, but is rejected; hell, in that Sartrian mode, is other people, and so on.
48. To some extent, this "detail" all but seals Iggy's fate.
49. This copper-fastens Iggy's demise.
50. Against a musical setting poignantly scored by Grieg, the murderous events are conveyed to the audience – who are effectively as blind at this point as most of the play's protagonists are throughout – by Mrs P.'s reactions.
51. The accidental death "verdict" certainly suits the Centre's rationale and life can go on. "Suicide" would have been bad for morale, and murder – which is what Mrs P. has witnessed – is simply unthinkable. So the story is that Iggy was killed while subterfugally practising alone on the toboggan run – an activity he should have undertaken with the others at the normal, stipulated time.
52. The reactions of some of the students to Iggy's death might be said to be unconvincingly accepting: Lisa is "unemotional" and quickly returns to Mikey's side; Jane and Charles seem to reunite in minutes.
53. With false subtlety, Mrs P. lets Iggy know that she is aware that he either stunned or killed Iggy before carrying him to the top of the toboggan tower and throwing him off. She has kept her eyes clamped on Charles from the moment the boys came back on stage with Iggy's corpse, and deals with him carefully, putting the Centre and its good before all other considerations. Charles rejects her (quasi-maternal) concern and affection, and any notion that his actions could have amounted to a crime of passion (to win back Jane).
54. The ultimate, Iggy-inspired alibi.
55. Here Buero-Vallejo tells his readers – although not the theatre audience – that Charles did, indeed, murder Iggy.

56. Having cruelly dismissed Mrs P. and her (over-)fondness for him, and with her words "You haven't won" ringing in his ears, the solitary, anxious Charles effectively becomes his victim, Iggy: in dress, movement, and – above all – speech, repeating Iggy's fine words from earlier in the Act. The final minutes of the play mark Iggy's triumph of sorts: Mrs P. recognises the validity of Iggy's insight ("only Iggy thought of that") and Charles has implicitly come to perceive the falseness of the Centre's normality.

Printed and bound by CPI Group (UK) Ltd, Croydon, CR0 4YY

13/04/2025

14656608-0002